Sacred Mysteries

Sacred Mysteries

The Human Face of Religion

CHRISTOPHER HOWSE

continuum

Continuum
The Tower Building, 11 York Road, London SE1 7NX
80 Maiden Lane, Suite 704, New York NY 10038

www.continuumbooks.com

First published 2007

British Library Cataloguing-in-Publication Data
A catalogue record for this book is available from the British Library.

ISBN 0-8264-9497-8

Typeset by Kenneth Burnley, Wirral, Cheshire
Printed and bound by MPG Books Ltd, Bodmin, Cornwall

Contents

Introduction		xi
1	**Ritual Animals**	**1**
	Night of Horror	1
	Fishless Fridays	2
	What's It Mean?	4
	Fenny Poppers	5
	Human Sacrifice	7
	Bundles of Herbs	9
	Key-belts	10
	No Leaven	12
	Beggars First	13
	Saint in a Box	15
	Old Bells	16
2	**From Long Ago**	**19**
	Place of Dread	19
	Art of Garnishing	21
	Up the Flagpole	22
	Abbey Burglar	24
	Wonder of the World	25
	No Dolls' Eyes	27
	A Secret People	28
	Our Own Charterhouse	30
	Letters on the Wall	32
	Cope Jealousy	33
	Lucky Strike	35
	Cathedral Charges	37

Contents

3 Inside Books   **39**
Mma Ramotswe's Morals   39
Ulfire and Jale   41
Brilliant Pages   42
Wesley's *Imitation*   44
Love's Laundry   45
The Suicide Club   47
Cherie on GKC   48

4 Talking with God   **51**
Prayers that Work   51
A Private Diary   53
What Anyone Can Do   55
God's Rescue Plan   56
Bowl of Cherries   58
A Lost Pet   59
Online   61
Lady Godiva's Chaplet   62
Muddled Psalms   63

5 Rites of Passage   **67**
In a Watery Grave   67
Brisbane's Fonts   69
Vision of Magnus   70
No Idolatry   72
Sister Death   73

6 Remarkable People   **77**
George Thomas of Soho   77
Canterbury Asian   79
A Saint to a Dinosaur   81
China's Marco Polo   82
Talking Eagle   84
Tragic-comic Life   85
A Barbastro Boy   87
Debt to the Poor   89
Sharp amid Disaster   90
Martyr in Greeneland   92

Contents

7 Living Creatures   **95**
  Food to Jump At   95
  Birds of Heaven   97
  Bats, not Rats   99
  Chickens in Church   100
  A Lion Footrest   101
  Elephant in the Tower   103
  Dogs Welcome   105
  Woodpecker's Dinner   107

8 Haphazard Hymns   **109**
  Hashish-drunk   109
  Bright or Wicked   111
  Jesus in the Womb   113
  The Bishops' Ban   114

9 Understanding Islam   **117**
  Ramadan   117
  Ten Things to Know   118
  The Sacrifice   121
  Scourged Shi'ites   122
  Saints' Shrines   124
  Presence of God   125
  An Old Game   127
  Intolerant Tolerance   129
  Not So Sunny   131
  Abraham's Religion   133

10 Brain Waves   **135**
  God Is   135
  Doubts of Chauntecleer   137
  Non-negotiable   138
  Sharing a Couch   140
  Trinity in Mind   142
  Trusting the Tongue   143
  Fundamental Foundations   145
  Cicero's Eternal Law   147
  Is Sex Love?   148

Contents

11 Last Things   **151**

Return from the Grave   151

Soul and Body   153

A Song to the End   154

The Victorian Way   156

The Death of the Pope   158

Getting Out of Hell   160

Trees of Armageddon   161

All About Rapture   163

Index   167

For Maurice Lipsedge
who is always interested

Introduction

The discovery that some churches in Britain still preserve pairs of tongs which wardens once used to remove quarrelsome dogs is hardly the key to religion. To those who have some interest in history it is, however, a point worthy of note. The small details of worship tell us something about the worshippers and their beliefs, just as in secular life their skirts and breeches, wigs and hats, meat and drink, coaches and footpaths, candles and shutters tell of a habit of mind as well as an economic system of existence. The Saturday columns from *The Daily Telegraph* collected in this book are certainly not meant as spiritual meditations. Nor are they contributions to theological debate. Largely they focus on odds and ends of religious life: historical survivals, unusual practices, peculiar people.

These phenomena do not add up to religion. They are like the corona round the sun that is visible during an eclipse. The sun itself is too bright to look at but when it is covered by the moon, at least we can see the effects of its burning activity. God is invisible and human characters, sacred buildings, art, music and literature at best throw out a little of the light taken from him in whom they thrive. Anyway, there is in one sense no such thing as religion. Some religions are bad. Some must be false in some aspects, since they contradict aspects of other religions. The philosopher William Charlton has remarked that religions are less like kinds of dog than kinds of duke. The idea of a duke for someone in Britain is very different from the idea of a duke for an Eskimo.

For all that, 'Man is a ritual animal', as the anthropologist Mary Douglas has observed. From her own study and analysis of the cult of the pangolin, or scaly anteater, among the Lele people of the Congo, she could not help drawing parallels with Christian beliefs. 'In their descriptions of the pangolin's behaviour and in their attitude to its cult', she wrote in *Purity and Danger* (1966),

'Lele say things which uncannily recall passages of the Old Testament, interpreted in the Christian tradition. Like Abraham's ram in the thicket and like Christ, the pangolin is spoken of as a voluntary victim. It is not caught, but rather it comes to the village. It is a kingly victim: the village treats its corpse as a living chief and requires the behaviour of respect for a chief on pain of future disaster. If its rituals are faithfully performed, the women will conceive and animals will enter hunters' traps and fall to their arrows. The mysteries of the pangolin are sorrowful mysteries: "Now I will enter the house of affliction," they sing as initiates carry its corpse round the village.'

Now, to anthropologists as a class of scientist, all systems of behaviour must remain entirely relative. They cannot say that westerners see things as they really are and funny foreigners are as mistaken in their apprehensions as they are different in their customs. But shake off the discipline of social science, and the observation of strange practices, like the experience of foreign travel, illuminates not only the foreigner but also one's own system of beliefs. If the observer believes in God as the creator of all things, then it will not seem unreasonable to find in alien religious life some hint of the spiritual, moral, cultic and conceptual aspects of the religion the observer knows so well.

We must beware, though, for we easily mistake the significance even of our own of rituals, and more so those of other people. When Samuel Pepys went out of curiosity to a synagogue in the 1660s he was shocked to 'see the disorder, laughing, sporting and no attention, but confusion in all their service, more like Brutes than people knowing the true God'. What he did not know was that the day he went was the festival of Simchat Torah, 'The Rejoicing for the Law', observed with free expression of cheerfulness. Pepys's misinterpretation was like a man from China today coming upon a church where pets are blessed on St Francis's day and concluding that donkeys and cats played an essential part in Christian rites. Or, to the shame of anthropologists, it was like western observers thinking that 'primitive' people expected rain-rituals to produce rain, when the people under observation realized perfectly well that their rituals were set for the season when rain would come, and their ceremonies marked the blessed gift, but did not bring it about.

Such mistakes happen closer to home. We don't know what we've got till it's gone. In 1967, kindly bishops in England and Wales decided that it would be easier for Catholics not to have to go to the trouble of abstaining from meat on Fridays. 'Non-Catholics know and accept that we do not eat meat on Fridays, but often they do not understand why we do not,' they said in an official explanation. But did the bishops? Certainly fasting or abstinence was a participation in the sufferings of Jesus on the day of his Crucifixion, and a reminder that many of our brothers and sisters in this world do not have enough to eat. It was also an unappreciated marker, a bond between co-religionists. Its abolition had the opposite effect to that intended: it made self-denial just one more lifestyle choice, like dieting or buying organic eggs. It made adherence to a religion more difficult, not easier, for it dissolved the bonds of common purpose and isolated the believer.

Fishless Fridays are not the end of the world. But the uprooting of ritual in church has accompanied decline in the European West of popular churchgoing. It was true that the language of the Book of Common Prayer or Coverdale's *Psalms* did not chime in with modern speech. It was true that people at Mass did not understand what was going on at the altar. But did churchgoers want the sacral language of worship to mimic the language of the office or the television? Did Massgoers expect the rites of the ineffable God to be understandable like a lecture in citizenship? Liturgy comes from a word meaning 'public work'; by its performance more is expressed than can be conveyed in verbal formulae. Like music, liturgy holds more than can be explained in a commentary. The meaning is implicit and conveyed by performance. It is not a theatrical performance but more like the performance of a string quartet, not in its aesthetics, but in the thing behind the music. Or it is like the performance of daily tasks in a family. If you ask, 'What do you mean by breakfast?' the answer is unlikely to explain the implicit bonds of care, love, give and take, unresolved tensions and growth to maturity inherent in consuming yoghurt and toast and coffee against the clock while getting the children to school on time without ignoring their preoccupations. Very likely worshippers didn't think in explicit terms about the problem of reinventing liturgy, or perhaps they feared to seem unprogressive and unmodern. In the same generation when families stopped sitting round tables for meals, many of them stopped going to church.

There are plenty of other reasons that many have stopped going to church. One is that people feel cut off from the weight of history stacked up in the form of church buildings, artefacts and writings. The sort of thing that comes to mind if you mention churchgoing is stained glass, which hardly anyone has in his house. I have always thought it odd that commentaries on old churches speak of stained glass as the Bible of the poor, that is, storytelling for the illiterate. Yet, as anyone who has gone round a church with a companion who is unfamiliar with the Bible will recognize, the windows, even if they can be seen clearly, will mean very little to those without a prior knowledge of the story of David and Bathsheba, of Abraham and the ram caught by its horns, of the burning bush, of the massacre of the innocents, of the flight into Egypt or the harrowing of hell. The whole of church architecture suffers the same difficulty, to a greater degree. Why should there be an openwork screen between nave and chancel? Why are reredoses or altarpieces so often of Victorian manufacture? Why is the lectern in the shape of an eagle? What happens at the altar? Look at the old brasses that people love to rub: why are tigers depicted on them shown with mirrors, and what does a panther signify? None of this is self-explanatory. It is like going into a betting-shop for the first time. Irishmen in overcoats, with nicotine-stained fingers, know what the form-guide (or holy-water stoup) is for, without any instruction. The deculturated need instruction, and they do not know what it is that they are ignorant of.

The case is reinforced by so many survivals from past centuries literally being museum pieces. I describe in this book a medieval embroidery in Girona that is one of the wonders of the world. It is kept in a museum attached to the cathedral, and although the images it bears are not recondite, you would have to know, for example, that the figures pouring out water represent the four rivers of paradise. The helpful explanatory labels sewn into the embroidery by its makers are all in Latin, and people do not understand Latin. So the impression is built up, here and elsewhere, that, though undeniably beautiful, the legacy of

Christianity is obscure, irrelevant, directed to other interests than our own, and preserved behind locked doors for the benefit of historians.

Fortunately the process can be reversed. Many British people like looking around old churches, even if they are atheists. They find the aesthetics, learning and motives of distant generations fascinating. And they learn that people at the time of Thomas Becket, or Bede, or Jerome, were not dirty, crude, ignorant or undiscerning. Indeed their insights into the teachings of Christianity do not contradict but amplify the narrow horizons of present-day searchers after truth. Simply to look at the beauty of the Lindisfarne Gospels or the mosaics at Ravenna is to begin to apprehend a world that wanted to express transcendent ideas in a superlative way. If what we see from past centuries delights the eye, then what we read makes us think again. It is a surprise and a matter of some interest to discover, for example, that from the time of St Hilary in the fourth century, Christian divines exerted their minds in considering the nine months that Jesus spent in the womb before his birth; to Eastern writers particularly it was part of the process by which he took on himself our nature so that we should be divinized by him.

So if I seem to rummage through ancient curiosities in some of the articles collected here, it is out of an interest in the way people arranged their lives in lost worlds, but it is also because it seems to me that we bring back from unfamiliar ages a critique and supplement to our own habits of mind.

In any case, we are not just pitching camp in the mud surrounding the ruins of a lost Christian civilization. The numbers who still do go to church are not negligible. Two million or so go regularly to Church of England services; a million or more to Catholic Masses on Sundays; Methodists and Nonconformists count for thousand upon thousand more. Migrants from Africa have set up their own thriving churches; migrants from Poland have swelled extant congregations. It is not, though, numbers that are always significant. There are fewer than two million Muslims in Britain, yet Islam is of great interest to us at the moment because we find Muslims amongst us who have formed a strong identity based on religion. We see wars in the Middle East and Afghanistan that involve Muslims. We have experienced the effects of terrorism motivated by a politicized interpretation of Islam. So suddenly we want to know what Islam is really about, when before, like the rules of bridge or mastery of the piano, it seemed too difficult to discover.

Islam, like Judaism and Christianity, is called an Abrahamic religion. In this I see hope, not a guarantee of conflict. Adherents of all three religions regard themselves as children of Abraham. Judaism is sometimes said to be a religion of law; others see it as a religion supported by behaviour among a people, passed on by imitation. Islam is full of law, too, and is said by some to have no room for theological speculation. What Christianity is depends on where you find it; what it should be is clearer, for its uncontroverted core is love, which it identifies with God.

The three Abrahamic religions believe in one God, and the same God, the living God of Abraham, Isaac and Jacob. Muslims fear that Christians do not believe in one God, since they worship Jesus as the Son of God. The same obstacle is apparent to Jews. The Christian is left having to affirm that he really does believe in one God, and not just one among many, but God who is so much one that his unity is stronger than any arithmetic designation. The Christian does not hope to explain the Trinity of God, for he protests that he did not invent the doctrine, it was revealed to him. With Augustine of Hippo, he says that we call the Trinity in God 'persons' *ne omnino taceretur*, 'lest otherwise we should fall silent'. Even Augustine, that restless mind searching for ways of talking about God, fell back upon crying, 'Holy, Holy, Holy'.

If the Christian cannot explain God and the Muslim continues to suspect that Christians believe in more than one God, then perhaps, away from theology, there is something that Jews, Christians and Muslims share in the practice of prayer. An Islamic devotion is the recitation of the 99 Names of God. Truly it is said that whoever enumerates them will get into paradise. That does not mean just listing them. By bringing them to mind, the devout person remembers God, draws near to him and with God's help follows his ordinances. These names include The All-Beneficent, The Merciful, The Sovereign, The Most Holy.

These are names we recognize. On our lips or in our minds they do not constrain God, who is more than we can say or conceive. In the Bible we read that Moses asked God who he was.

'And God said unto Moses, I AM THAT I AM: and he said, Thus shalt thou say unto the children of Israel, I AM hath sent me unto you. And God said moreover unto Moses, Thus shalt thou say unto the children of Israel, The LORD God of your fathers, the God of Abraham, the God of Isaac, and the God of Jacob, hath sent me unto you: this is my name for ever, and this is my memorial unto all generations' (Exod. 3.14).

Did Moses get the answer he hoped for? God told him he was 'I AM'. He told him he was the God of Abraham. Those statements are true, but still the name of God is unknowable, for God is not a kind of creature who has a name that defines him. He is who he is. The Jews would not, out of respect, speak the word that we pronounce as Yahweh. It is impossible to say God's own name, for only God knows God, and a name implies a knowledge of the nature of the one named. It is not just that we have not been told his name; we would not be able to hear it if we were told. Instead, God has revealed himself to us. That revelation is not written in a book, though a book contains revelation about him. Revelation is God communicating himself, not merely providing us with information. We give God the name Love. God is Love and love moves outwards. When we pray we say that we lift up our hearts and minds to God, but in reality we open ourselves to his action, which is an outpouring of love.

Anyone can pray, and the communion that God offers would make all the trivialities of breakfast and work and dog-tongs utterly despicable, were it not that God had entered into the world by taking flesh upon himself. No longer is it mankind in the world and the unknowable God transcendent and beyond our deepest yearnings. Instead, the world and its history are transformed from the inside. Prayer is now not an intellectual exercise, or a silent standing before utter otherness. Prayer becomes something still human, but which is done beside our brother Jesus Christ who taught us to say 'Our Father'. That is the Christian perspective, and it has changed the world.

Christopher Howse
Westminster, 2007

1
Ritual Animals

Night of Horror

I spent a night of Gothick horror in Mexico the other week, shut up in the mouldering remains of an old monastery in the hands of an unknown cult. I had naively followed a suggestion of stopping over on a Saturday night at what I was told was a retreat house at Atlixco, near the volcano of Popocatepetl. It was after dark when I arrived at the sixteenth-century former convent of San Francisco, and once the great wooden doors had been barred behind me I was led through a courtyard into a vaulted room where men and women in white robes were gathered around plates of food. 'It is Shabbat,' I was told. 'Join us.'

One thing I did know is that after dark on a Saturday is not Shabbat, which has finished by then. In any case, I was dog-tired and did not want to share the proffered fruit squash (which of course reminded me of Jonestown) for fear of the mundane problem of gastro-enteric infection. The politest thing I could do was to go to bed. The room I was taken to was empty save for four bunks and one chair. A yellowing curtain was drawn over the glassless window. The nearest lavatory was along dark, uncharted passageways. As I made myself as comfortable as a blanket and a flock pillow allowed, the sounds of the Mexican night settled in: dogs barking, car horns, screams, a disco, sirens. A cicada set up in competition in the corner of the room, and a mosquito circled in descant. I fell asleep with memories of Aldous Huxley and of Aztec rites of human sacrifice.

Early next morning, I joined the community in a big colonial church where they chanted morning prayer, with borrowings from the Greek Orthodox liturgy. Men stood at one side, women at the other. There was extemporary prayer, too, and some cried Alleluia, or groaned. Over a bread and mango breakfast, I learnt that this was the Community of the Beatitudes, founded only in the 1970s. It is recognized by the Roman Catholic Church. Its characteristics include a respectful interest in Jewish worship, openness to other Christians, a 'charismatic' element (worshipping with inspiration from the Holy Spirit). The three essentials are prayer, poverty and obedience. The central act is Eucharistic worship. I left that day with my night horrors dispelled, impressed by the sincerity and commitment of these mostly young people. I had known nothing of them before; there are 30 houses in France, none in Britain.

It strikes me that their mix is a new one. They are poor, spiritual, ecumenical, contemporary, open to the handicapped; but some of the framed pictures in their house showed saints usually connected with traditionally orientated Catholics: Padre Pio, St Thérèse of Lisieux, St Faustina Kowalska, St Louis-Marie Grignon de Montfort. Theirs is not a life I would like to share, but it is good to see new vigour in an old Christian country. It is a sort of radicalized tradition.

6 JULY 2002

Fishless Fridays

There is a sense that 'Sunday is no longer a "church" day for our society, but rather a family day or a DIY day, or sports club day or whatever people choose to do'. That observation, in a pamphlet called *Mission-Shaped Church* (Church House Publishing), has provoked newspaper reports that the C of E was considering the abolition of Sunday services.

Deranged as this suggestion might sound, almost no baby is at present safe from being thrown out with the bath water. After all, the Ten Commandments enjoin that the 'Sabbath' be kept holy, and Christians soon dropped Saturdays in favour of Sundays. 'The sabbath was made for man, not man for the sabbath,' as Jesus remarked.

In the same chapter of the Gospel according to St Mark, Jesus is asked in an accusing tone why his disciples don't fast. In his answer he predicts that when 'the bridegroom shall be taken away from them', then they'll fast. Jesus himself being the bridegroom, plainly.

This answer is picked up by Professor Eamon Duffy, the Cambridge historian, in a plea for the restoration of fasting. 'What was once a truly corporate observance', he writes in *The Tablet*, 'reminding us of the Passion of Christ, our own spiritual poverty and, even more concretely, of the material poverty of most of the human race, has become another individual consumer choice, like going on a diet.'

In 1967 the Catholic bishops of England and Wales made abstinence from meat on Fridays optional. It had been one of the most obvious markers of being a Catholic. Like the people who prefer to worship on other days instead of Sunday, the bishops saw good reasons for the decision to drop Friday abstinence. 'It is a question whether it is advisable in our mixed society', they said at the time, 'for a Catholic to appear singular in this matter. Non-Catholics know and accept that we do not eat meat on Fridays, but often they do not understand why we do not.'

No more did the bishops, so it seemed. And why should they? There are many traditional religious acts performed for no agreed reason. The Jews are forbidden to eat pork. Why? Out of obedience to an arbitrary rule, some said, or as a sort of parable not to imitate the behaviour pigs are thought to symbolize, said others. Moses Maimonides, the medieval commentator, looked for a practical reason – to avoid disease, perhaps.

The so-called abominations listed in the book of Leviticus (sea creatures without fins and scales, or the owl, the night-hawk and the cuckoo) were in our own times famously decoded by the anthropologist Mary Douglas in an essay later included in her book *Purity and Danger* (Routledge, 1966). Although she has adjusted her theories since, the study showed how the prohibitions of the Jewish law expressed the holiness and purity of God. Another of Mary Douglas's insights was into the very practice of not eating meat on Fridays. Her essay, 'The Bog Irish' (collected in *Natural Symbols*, Routledge, 1982), eloquently described a distinguishing feature of Irish Catholic life, as observable in Britain, of eating fish, or rather abstaining from meat, on Fridays as a sort of badge of membership.

To remove the prohibition of meat was intended to remove an awkward burden from folk's shoulders. Instead, the bog-standard Catholic, as it were, who knew no clearer sign of identity than this cultic dietary prohibition, felt more rootless and less willing to make the effort to observe the more weighty obligations of religion. The poor bishops had sold out just at the moment the anthropologists were riding to their rescue with an appreciation of what it was that they were casting aside.

Professor Duffy in his *Tablet* article does not take up Mary Douglas's theme, beyond agreeing that Friday abstinence was strictly observed by both 'good' and 'bad' Catholics. But he does call for a rededication to 'the observance of fasting and abstinence' voluntarily. Imagine the shock if episcopal authority attempted to reimpose a binding obligation.

7 FEBRUARY 2004

What's It Mean?

A surprise bestseller this autumn is *How to Read a Church* by Richard Taylor (Rider). Most people are shy, mystified and then quickly bored on entering a church. The great thing about Mr Taylor's book is to explain not so much the architectural as the theological function of the things inside. As nations depressingly persevere in war, the need is urgent to understand their national cultures and religions, which are not quite the same thing. There is plenty of scope for misinterpretation.

On 14 October 1663, six years after Jews re-established themselves in England, Pepys, open-eyed as ever, visited the synagogue in Creechurch Lane. 'Their service all in a singing, and in Hebrew,' he noted. 'Anon, their Laws, that they take out of the press, is carried by several men, four or five, several burthens in all, and they do relieve one another, or whether it is that everyone desires the carrying of it, I cannot tell. But, Lord, to see the disorder, laughing, sporting and no attention, but confusion in all their service, more like Brutes than people knowing the true God, would make a man forswear ever seeing them more; and indeed, I never did see so much, or could have imagined there had been any religion in the whole world so absurdly performed as this.'

Poor Pepys was extrapolating from insufficient information,

for he had hit without knowing it upon the festival Simchat Torah, 'The Rejoicing for the Law', observed by that Portuguese Sephardic community with unrestrained expressions of cheerfulness. This year it falls on 19 October.

It is as if some man from China had stumbled into a harvest festival service and concluded that Christians worshipped stooks of corn, or come across a church where pets are blessed on St Francis's day and supposed that donkeys and cats played an essential part in Christian rites. As it happens, Christians still misunderstand even each other so completely as almost to seem wilful. Protestants feel queasy when a Catholic kisses a saint's image, as if it were really idolatry. Ritualists are disgusted by guitars and extemporised 'liturgy'.

Perhaps worse is an untested assumption that all religions are 'really the same'. By the evidence of their practices, they most certainly are not. Pepys went away, his 'mind strangely disturbed'. If he had found out more, he might have been less upset.

27 SEPTEMBER 2003

Fenny Poppers

It's Fenny Poppers today. I mean that, as well as the solemn day of Remembrance, today has long been marked at Fenny Stratford in Buckinghamshire as the day to set off six small cast-iron cannons, with the help of a long iron with a red-hot tip, at noon, two o'clock and four. Once upon a time the cannonade was fired in the churchyard of St Martin's church, but it seems that the parish feared for the safety of its structure, and the event was moved to a nearby recreation ground. St Martin's day falls today, of course – the day when pigs were killed and puddings boiled – but you won't find that the Fenny Poppers date back to the merrieness of medieval times.

They were most likely instituted by the eccentric antiquary Browne Willis (1682–1760), in memory of his grandfather, who had lived in St Martin's Lane in London and died on St Martin's day. Willis was a serious historian and from 1724, as the local squire, paid for the church to be rebuilt, in gothic, not the

5

fashionable neo-classical style. But Willis looked odd. In middle age he had 'more the appearance of a mumping beggar than a gentleman – dressed in an old slouched hat, more brown than black, a weather-beaten large wig, three or four old-fashioned coats, all tied round by a leather belt, and over all an old blue cloak, lined with black'.

I found the Fenny Poppers in the splendid, fat, illustrated *The English Year* (Penguin), a good Christmas-present candidate by Steve Roud. The refreshing thing about Mr Roud is that he does not pass on ill-founded received ideas about festivals. This is particularly notable in connection with customs reputed to date back to pagan times. 'Hallowe'en is probably the most widely misunderstood and misrepresented day in the festival year,' he says, for example. 'But so many now believe that it was originally a pagan festival of the dead that the belief is virtually impossible to shake. The facts, however, are very different.'

It was a Christian festival inaugurated in the medieval period, he explains. 'There is no evidence that this time of year was celebrated in England before the Christian feast was created.' In Ireland, 1 November was 'Samhain', the beginning of winter, but 'not, it seems, of much religious or supernatural significance'.

For the English, apart from the ordinary celebration of All Saints on 1 November and All Souls the next day, that time of year came in some parts of the country to be marked as Mischief Night, with practical jokes played, such as untethering a horse from a cart while its owner was in the pub, and reattaching horse and cart on either side of a gateway, with the shafts poking through the gate. Very amusing.

In other parts of the country Mischief Night was on 4 November, the Eve of Guy Fawkes, or May Day Eve, 30 April. The latter is familiar to us, at least since the time of Goethe, who mentions it in *Faust* (1823) as Walpurgisnacht, the eve of the feast of the translation of the relics of St Walburga, a companion of St Boniface of Crediton in the conversion of Germany in the eighth century.

'Soon it will be Walpurgis Night,' says the publisher's blurb to Dennis Wheatley's *The Irish Witch*. 'Soon a ruined castle will echo to the baying of initiates as Susan is led towards an altar – there to be ritually violated by the Priest of Satan.' This is typical of

Wheatley's invention, and no tradition of this being a night for witches was ever known in England or indeed Ireland, unlike Germany. Even there the Wheatley-like details of pagan rites never pertained.

May Eve is, however, the night on which the action of Shakespeare's *Midsummer Night's Dream* is set. 'No doubt they rose up early to observe/The rite of May,' says Theseus of the young people found asleep. So fairies might be expected to be about. The people of Kingstone and Thruxton in Herefordshire once used kindly to leave trays of moss outside their doors for the fairies to dance upon. But this is a folk belief rather than a persistence of some pagan system of the sort invented by the father of Wicca, Gerald Gardner, as long ago as 1954.

11 NOVEMBER 2006

Human Sacrifice

In June 2005, the London *Evening Standard* carried a front-page headline: 'Children sacrificed in London churches, say police'. A reporter on the BBC's *Today* programme said there were 'countless examples of children being beaten, even murdered after being identified as witches by pastors'. The accusations were made about African churches. But what was the truth of them?

The torso of a little boy was found in the Thames in 2001, and police said they thought he had died in a ritualistic killing; 300 African boys had gone missing in London in three months, they said. The year before, Victoria Climbié had been murdered with horrible cruelty. More recently a little girl thought to be a witch was abused with much cruelty. The temptation is to conclude that 'African' beliefs have led to abuse and murder, some perpetrated by worshippers at unregulated churches. But do the crimes derive from one trend and indicate a horrifically larger picture of unsolved abuse and killing?

The dead boy in the Thames, named Adam by investigators, was thought to have come from Nigeria, but the sort of crime suspected is connected with the preparation of magical medicine, or muti, as practised in South Africa. In Soweto, 300 boys were thought to have been killed in a decade and parts of their bodies used in such 'medicine'; their mutilated bodies were found on waste ground. But this is not 'sacrifice', though the murders were disgusting.

Apart from Adam, no such corpses have been found in London. Police do not suggest that the 300 boys missing from school are victims of anything more sinister than unnotified movement, bureaucratic confusion or benefit fraud. A psychiatrist I spoke to, who has specialised in the field of ethnic belief and practice for many years, said he had come across all sorts of strange, sometimes alarming, behaviour, but not child sacrifice.

Muti killings are a completely different category of behaviour from the victimization of people believed to be witches. Victoria Climbié was abused before she was ever taken to a 'black' church. In the case of the abused Angolan girl beaten as a witch, a woman convicted of her harm had been expelled from the church she attended.

There is evidence that among some people from the Democratic Republic of Congo, children are sometimes held to be 'witches', or thought to have a substance inside them that is malevolent, from which they are delivered by imposed fasts and pummelling. Writing in the *Church Times* last week of black churches that make deliverance from witchcraft a central point of belief, Professor Paul Gifford, of the School of Oriental and African Studies, said: 'Deliverance is often carried out in an atmosphere of drama, frenzy and intense physicality. Sometimes it involves pummelling those possessed, although I doubt that I have ever witnessed anything that would cause the police to intervene.'

To attribute a single belief about witchcraft to all Africans is ludicrously misconceived. In his classic study of beliefs among a tribe who live in southern Sudan and Congo, *Witchcraft among the Azande*, E. E. Evans-Pritchard showed how belief in witchcraft answered a question unplumbed in the developed West: why a mishap should fall on me particularly. The Azande did not necessarily blame 'witches' for provoking bad events, since the effect could be performed involuntarily. The easiest way of dealing with a witch was to go to meet him and ask him to stop. Children were the least likely to be suspected of being witches.

I am not saying that Azande beliefs about witchcraft are true. But their beliefs were integrated into an open, well-regulated society. Other African cultures attribute misfortune to personal guilt or to the inscrutable acts of God.

The great paradox is that we in the West accuse Africans of wickedness in seeking out witches, while we are blind to the equally irrational witch-hunt that has been launched against African churches by British people prepared to believe the worst, no matter how improbable.

15 OCTOBER 2005

Bundles of Herbs

The Popish Kingdom or Reign of Antichrist is not the kind of title that one comes across in publishers' catalogues these days. But the identification of the Pope with Antichrist was an unexceptionable commonplace in respectable Protestant circles until well into the nineteenth century. I am not quite sure what led to its decline; biblical textual criticism perhaps overshadowed the question.

When I came across this energetic title, I had not been pursuing the theme of Antichrist, but the doctrine of the Assumption of the Blessed Virgin Mary. The Assumption figures in some verses from *The Popish Kingdom* quoted in the excellent *Oxford Companion to the Year*, edited by Bonnie Blackburn and Leofranc Holford-Strevens. I had never seen a copy of *The Popish Kingdom*, and on finding out more I realized why.

It was written by Barnaby Googe and published in 1570, but by the nineteenth century only one complete copy was known to be in existence, perhaps a sign that instead of being bought for the shelf, it was enthusiastically read to bits. Googe did not make it up out of his own head, but translated it from a work by a man called Thomas Kirchmeyer, who had Grecianized his surname as Naogeorgus. (It was a fashionable practice; the resounding Oecolampadius, for example, came from a family called Hausschein.)

Anyway, Googe was of a mind with Naogeorgus about papistical practices, and by good fortune he has left us details unrecorded elsewhere of many folk customs that he deplored. Here he is on the evil concomitants of the Assumption:

The blessed virgin Maries feast hath here his place and
  time,
Wherein departing from the earth, she did the heavens
  clime;
Great bundles then of hearbes to Church, the people fast
  doe beare,
The which against all hurtfull things, the Priest doth hallow
  theare.
Thus kindle they and nourish still, the peoples
  wickednesse,
And vainely make them to believe, whatsoever they
  expresse;
For sundrie witchcrafts by those hearbes are wrought, and
  divers charmes,
And cast into the fire are thought to drive away all harmes.

The verse form of 'fourteeners', long lines capable of being
scanned as ballad metre, like the poem *John Gilpin*, was used by
good and bad poets of the time. Googe is no good versifier.
But the point of interest here is that he does not denounce the
doctrine of the Assumption itself, but what seem to him wickedly
superstitious customs surrounding its celebration. The people
are using the herbs, he suggests, in an apotropaic way, to drive
away evil as if they had any virtue in themselves. Those who
observed the custom would have defended it as a sort of sacramental, like sprinkling blessed water.

However that may be, the Book of Common Prayer did not
incorporate the feast of the Assumption. But in 1997 the Church
of England added to its calendar a Festival of the Blessed Virgin
Mary on 15 August.

10 AUGUST 2002

Key-belts

I had not considered the use of key-belts until I read a very jolly
article in the *Jewish Chronicle*. A Shabbat key-belt is for many a
necessary accessory. The problem it addresses is that the Jewish
law forbids not only gainful labour on the sabbath but also carry-

ing things, such as keys, from one house to another. So how are you to get back indoors after coming back from the synagogue? One answer has been the key-belt. This is not a belt on which keys may be hung. That would not comply with the law. The keys have to be an essential part of the structure of the belt. Thus you do not carry the keys, you wear them, as a link that keeps together the belt around your waist.

But now in Hendon, north London, which boasts a high number of Jews, they have constructed an eruv. An eruv is an altogether more compendious way of getting round sabbath restrictions. It is a border round an area that designates it your home domain, in which pushing a child's buggy, picking up a prayer-book or a bunch of keys is not forbidden. The boundaries of the eruv in Hendon stretch for 11 miles, in places marked merely with nylon fishing-line linking tall poles. 'My first Shabbat in Hendon was bliss,' Nathan Jeffay says in his informative article on key-belts. 'A bottle of drink in hand during my weekend stroll and . . . laces in all my shoes.'

Mr Jeffay had formerly made a habit of sacrificing his laces to rig up a home-made key-belt. Now there is no need. But that leaves the manufacturers of key-belts in a worrying position. 'Demand is very low at the moment,' says Ezriel Cohen of Edgware, a belt-maker since the age of 12. 'There used to be good money in Shabbat belts, but not any more.'

From one viewpoint, key-belts seem to have about as much to do with religion as shamrock key-rings. Indeed, I know some secularized Jews who were driven to distraction in their youth by the stringencies and evasions of the sabbath. But for believers they may be a way of expressing faith in the lawgiver; getting round the prohibitions is for them not the same as rejecting them.

One odd thing is that, although they are common in the diaspora, key-belts are apparently rare in Israel, since it has eruvs all over the place. Another is that Mr Cohen the belt-maker is pictured in the *Jewish Chronicle* wearing braces. Perhaps they are held together with keys.

26 JULY 2003

No Leaven

Passover this year is out of the ordinary. It falls on 24 April, and the eve is a Saturday, the Sabbath or Shabbat. Usually the eve of Passover is the day for searching for anything containing leaven and burning it, and for preparing the Passover meal or Seder. But this is prohibited on the Sabbath. In trying to discover how the problem is solved, I became aware of how little I know of the laws and vocabulary familiar to Orthodox Jews in this country. So I shall probably get something wrong, for all my efforts.

In Jewish timekeeping (inherited by Christians when they start celebrations of feasts on the evening before), days begin at sunset. So, next Thursday, after nightfall, the search for chametz will begin. Chametz, literally 'leaven' or 'yeast', includes any kind of grain product (wheat, barley, oats, rye or spelt) on which water has acted more than 18 minutes before baking. The intention is to comply with the Passover injunction in the book of Exodus (13.7): 'There shall no leavened bread be seen with thee, neither shall there be leaven seen with thee in all thy quarters.'

The chametz is to be burnt by 11.48 next Friday morning (this representing, in London, the sixth hour of the solar day). But, in contrast to normal years, some chametz is kept back to be eaten on Friday evening and Saturday morning. Normally, at the burning of chametz, a declaration called the Kol Chamira is recited, annulling the ownership of any chametz; but this year, since some is kept back, the recitation is delayed till Saturday morning.

The Sabbath meal should be prepared on Friday and left in utensils dedicated to use for Pesach or Passover food. These are separate from dishes and utensils used ordinarily. Most people advise using paper plates this year, for they certainly cannot be washed on the Sabbath in preparation for the Passover.

On Friday, the eve of the Sabbath, challoth, bread, should be placed on a separate side table, on paper plates, with a mat on the floor to catch any crumbs. It should be kept well away from Pesach utensils. Bread should not be eaten after 10.36 on the Saturday morning. Paper plates should be thrown away outside. Great care has to be taken to get rid of any crumbs or leftover bread. A non-Jew could take away leftovers. On the eve of Pesach, as usual, no matzo, or unleavened bread, may be eaten either. One is supposed to be hungry for the Passover meal (though not fasting to the extent of discomfort).

Nothing may be done for the preparation of the Seder, the Passover meal, until the end of the Sabbath, at 9.02pm on Saturday, in London. Then the Yom Tov ('Good Day' or festival) candles may be lit from existing flames. This supposes the candles have kept burning from Friday. Then the family can sit down to the Seder. Hooray!

The London Beth Din, the religious court, publishes a list of products that are kosher for Passover. Apart from the ordinary prohibitions, they must contain no leaven. Danger lurks not only in foodstuffs, but also in toothpaste or products for chapped lips – Chap Stick is OK, but not the grape-flavour ones. Babies can't be given gripe water on Pesach, but Imodium for diarrhoea is fine.

You can't really blame the religious authorities for making the choice of Passover products so complicated. It's commercial production of food that has become complicated – not just e-numbers, but all the stuff shoved into food that no home cook would dream of using. I can see that a run-through of Sabbath and Passover prohibitions can seem like obsessive legalism. One hears from some secularized Jews that they have turned away from empty obligations and laws. And who could deny that empty formalism accompanied by an evil heart is despicable? But what about a good heart, in one who makes Passover different from any other night?

16 APRIL 2005

Beggars First

Almsgiving is the most problematical of the three practices – prayer, fasting and almsgiving – enjoined upon Christians in the six weeks of Lent, which begins next Wednesday. A widespread feeling is that donating money to a charity such as Oxfam or Cafod is praiseworthy but lacks the human touch; giving money to beggars is human but often neither good for them (they might buy drink) nor effective. (Why should the beggar on the doorstep benefit when the hidden pauper goes without?) City-goers hardly know if they pity or hate beggars.

Newman, in a bravura passage in his *Anglican Difficulties*, sought to *épater* godless respectability: 'Take a mere beggar-woman, lazy, ragged, filthy, and not over-scrupulous of truth – but if she is chaste, and sober, and cheerful, and goes to her religious duties – she will, in the eyes of the Church, have a prospect of heaven quite closed and refused to the State's pattern-man, the just, the upright, the generous, the honourable, the conscientious, if he be all this, not from a supernatural power – but from mere natural virtue.'

Certainly, Victorian travellers to Europe with their *Baedekers* and *Murray's Handbooks* saw and despised dirty, wheedling beggars, at a time when begging was criminal in England. Somehow, it seemed to Victorians, Lazarus at the gate or King Wenceslas's poor man must have comported themselves in a more agreeable manner.

A sort of emblematic beggar from another era is described in an anthropological study of Old Castile in the 1950s by Michael Kenny called *A Spanish Tapestry*. In the upland village that he calls Ramosierra, near Soria, each 17 August (the third day of the local feast), itinerant beggars would go from door to door crying their greeting. If those at home answered 'Who is it?' the answer would be 'Un pobre' – a poor man. He would be given food, clothing or money. The police would not interfere with such proud beggars, only moving on 'whining' beggars or gypsies.

So that is an 'acceptable' beggar. There is nothing especially medieval in this. The poor of the Middle Ages neither wallowed in Monty Python mud nor lived in amity with sturdy ploughmen and hospitable monks. In fourteenth-century England, socio-economics was a surprisingly popular subject for poetry. Some time after 1350 an anonymous poet wrote a verse debate called *Winner and Waster*, on the morality of labour and idle consumption; it might today have been entitled *Producer and Consumer*. The beggar, like the rich lordling, might be categorized as a useless consumer. Today, in a more humane spirit, it can cheer an almsgiver to get to know a beggar or *Big Issue* seller by name and follow his progress from hostel to bedsit.

9 FEBRUARY 2002

Saint in a Box

The mortal remains of St Thérèse of Lisieux are in Iraq, an unlikely place, since the saint died in France, aged 24, in 1897. But they are not staying. St Thérèse's relics, encased in a large, ornate chest, have been travelling the world since 1994 – a strange fate for a woman who resolved to spend all her adult life enclosed behind the walls of a Carmelite convent, praying for those outside whom she never met.

Starting with a trip to Lyons, the ancient capital of Christian Gaul, the relics had by 1997 reached Rome, where, suitably enough, Pope John Paul declared the saint a Doctor of the Church, a title bestowed on great teachers such as the fifth-century Augustine of Hippo, and also on Thérèse's Carmelite namesake, St Teresa of Avila (1515–82).

Since then, the relics have clocked up an impressive mileage, touring Brazil, with its 100 million Catholics, for a whole year, and making visits to Slovenia, Switzerland, Holland, the Philippines, 20 or 30 cities in America, as well as less obvious destinations such as Kazakhstan (for a month in 1999) and Vietnam (in 2000). Huge numbers turned out in Ireland during an 11-week tour in 2001.

The itinerary is organized by the shrine at Lisieux where the relics are venerated when not on tour. The relics were welcomed to Iraq by Archbishop Jean Slieman, the head of the Latin-rite Catholics in Baghdad. Iraq has about 800,000 Christians. Perhaps 400,000 others left the country in the decade after the Gulf war of 1990–91. Most of those remaining belong to the Chaldean Catholic Patriarchal Church, which has 40 parishes in Baghdad alone. Another concentration is in Mosul. These Chaldeans are in communion with Rome and have their own ancient liturgy. The language of worship is Syriac, a kind of Aramaic, the very language that Jesus spoke.

The relics of St Thérèse have not only been venerated by Christians, but, according to a spokesman for the Carmelite nuns, have also been accorded 'traditional signs of respect and celebration by Muslims'. Iraq is ruled by a secular regime, but the majority of the population are Shi'a Muslims.

Why, though, should the custodians of the relics want to send them all about the world? The saint herself often expressed her desire to spread the Christian Gospel. 'I should like to travel over the whole earth,' she wrote. 'I should like to be a missionary.'

Shortly before Thérèse's death, France passed a law forbidding burial within a convent's enclosure, and so pilgrims were able to begin visiting her grave at the town cemetery. The rationale for the veneration of her relics is the same as for that given to the reputed remains of St James at Santiago or those of St Nicholas (Santa Claus) at Bari. Pilgrims ask the saint in heaven to pray to God for them.

Next year there are plans for the relics to go to Scotland.

7 DECEMBER 2002

Old Bells

This week I learned the remarkable fact that whenever the Queen hears the bells of Westminster Abbey, she is listening to at least two that rang out for Elizabeth I. The Whitechapel Bell Foundry, a company still in operation, hung them there in 1583, and they have been rung ever since.

Bells go with Christmas and with the New Year. They have a place both in Christian worship and in state occasions. Perhaps for that reason, they have survived and flourished more healthily in England than anywhere else. Whenever Elizabeth I was taken by boat from Westminster Palace to Greenwich, or upstream to Richmond, the bells of Lambeth parish church, over the river, had to ring out. Each time, the bellringers were paid three shillings between them.

In 1598 Paul Hentzner, a member of the entourage of a Silesian nobleman visiting London, noted the behaviour of English bellringers. 'A number of them who have got a glass in their hands', he wrote, 'would go up into some belfry and ring the bells for hours together, for the sake of exercise.'

Today, there are about 40,000 regular bellringers in Britain. What makes their pastime so absorbing is not so much the beer as the change-ringing, which is the particular glory of the English belfry. Since the seventeenth century, bells have been mounted on wheels, and this enables a set of bells, tuned to a musical scale, to ring in time through a mathematical knitting-pattern of combinations. It sounds like nothing else, always harmonious but never picking out a tune in the way we expect from Bach. Foreign bells are well enough in their way. Often cracked, and sounded with an electric clapper, they ring the people to church or mark the passing of night, thus becoming part of the fabric of daily life. Worse, Belgian town councils make them ring tunes on the hour in carillons.

In England, church bells survived by accident, like copes, cathedral choirs, the sign of the Cross at baptism, organs, the dedication of churches to obscure saints and other unscriptural customs. By the time of Dickens, they went with mouldering tombstones in the churchyard, fading hatchments, moth-eaten military colours and the dusty cushion on the pulpit's edge for the parson's Prayer Book.

Dickens lived like a sort of Robinson Crusoe amid the chance wreckage of the Church of England, before its violent restoration during the liftetime of Queen Victoria. In 1844, the year after the success of *A Christmas Carol*, he published *The Chimes*. Though included in his *Christmas Books*, this was a tale of New Year's Eve.

Its protagonist is a poor, casual street porter who makes his living outdoors. (His appearance in his ragged porter's apron was brilliantly evoked by a regular illustrator of Dickens, John Leech.) He is so downtrodden that to him a windy day is welcome because it is an Event. He is nicknamed Trotty Veck, but, Dickens tells us, he was christened Toby. Dickens knew that ancient church bells had once been blessed with holy water and given names, and he insists that Toby Veck had 'been as lawfully christened in his day as the Bells had been in theirs, though with not quite so much of solemnity or public rejoicing'.

From the first, Toby Veck is depicted as being sympathetic to the church bells. He hears in them hope for the future: 'Toby Veck, Toby Veck, job coming soon, Toby! Toby Veck, Toby Veck, job coming soon, Toby!' The rest of the story deals with a dream that Toby Veck has, after a dinner of tripe and potatoes (like Scrooge after too much cheese). The dream is of despair, poverty, prostitution. The baddies are the Poor Law officials and utilitarian manufacturers. For them, the bells are useless and unproductive. There is a happy ending. Against the odds, church bells have happily survived everything: the changes in religion and the twentieth-century decline in churchgoing. They still suggest the transcendent, and our connection with it. Towards the end of a poem on prayer that gives a catalogue of images, George Herbert memorably suggests that prayer itself is 'Church-bells beyond the stars heard'.

24 DECEMBER 2005

2

From Long Ago

Place of Dread

At the Charterhouse of Miraflores, near Burgos, a beautiful stone screen spans the church, and over the doorway in it are carved '*Hic est domus Dei et porta caeli*' – this is the house of God and the gate of heaven. The words come from the mouth of Jacob, when, having taken a stone for a pillow, he has awoken from the dream that showed him the ladder reaching to heaven (Gen. 28.17). They are preceded by his exclamation, 'Surely the Lord is in this place, and I knew it not. How dreadful is this place!' He was afraid, with a sort of awe. When Jacob has recovered his power to act, he sets up the stone that was his pillow and pours oil on it. He calls the place Bethel – the House of God.

How does this compare with the way people regard churches today? They often say, and rightly, that a church is the gathering of the people of God, an *ecclesia*. The difference that it makes to its members is another thing, but what about the actual building that the local church has built for itself?

Most towns and villages in England (Scotland, Wales and Ireland being different stories) still have a church that was built hundreds of years ago. When it was consecrated to God, its stones would have been anointed with oil, like Jacob's pillow. It was made Bethel, the House of God.

For Christians, God's house is also Bethlehem, the House of Bread, for it is the place made holy, set aside, for the celebration of the Eucharist. It is the Eucharist that makes the church, the assembly of the people of God. It is the bread that has come down from heaven, as Jacob saw the angels ascending and descending on the ladder that reached from heaven to earth, the *porta caeli*. This bread is Emmanuel – God with Us. The Lord is in this place.

The church remains the House of God even when the

Eucharist is not being celebrated. It is difficult to know what we mean when we say that a place and the stones that make it up are holy. Of course they are set aside for God, so profane use is the breaking of a sacred covenant with God.

There is a memorable passage in Laurie Lee's book *A Rose for Winter* about fighting with the Republicans in the Spanish Civil War. His unit is billeted in a church one night, and the author boldly sleeps on the altar. It was something he regretted ever after.

If holiness is something not to be contravened, is it also something that rubs off, as it were? It is hard to see how, if the words of Jesus are to be taken seriously, about it being not externals but those bad things within a man, in his heart, that defile him. Contrariwise, goodness depends not on externals, but the heart.

Still, we are creatures made not only of flesh but also of the associations that have made the world in which we find ourselves: the history and culture of our people. If we are lucky enough to live where people like us have lived for a long time, we inherit the culture they made. It only takes a few years for a church building to acquire the discernible character of being a house of prayer. Naturally, attachment to human traditions – to armorial hatchments, regimental banners, even to bells and flower arrangements – can engender Pharisaism, that is, love of externals while the heart remains corrupt. Disgust with such Pharisaism drove hot prophets such as the seventeenth-century Quaker George Fox to despise church buildings as 'steeple houses'.

But the Church is not unaware of the danger, and reconciles the dead stones of the church building and the living stones of the Christians who make up its people. One of the prayers for the anniversary of the dedication of a church says: 'Here you build the spiritual temple which we are.'

Each Christian is a living stone, a portable temple of the Holy Spirit. It is at church that they build up the Body of Christ which they mystically constitute. Analogically the altar is Jesus's body too, which is why people bow to it, and the priest kisses it as he approaches to celebrate the Eucharist.

All this is far from a meeting hall also handy for coffee mornings.

16 SEPTEMBER 2006

Art of Garnishing

An energetic combination of cheerfulness, vulgarity, commercialism and piety is to be found in a strange secondhand book I've just come across called *The Art of Garnishing Churches at Christmas and Other Festivals*, published in 1869. It tells you how to transform a church by the simple means of lathes, iron rods, wire, perforated zinc, artificial flowers, cut-outs in cardboard, shapes in straw, gold paper, berries and greenery. Every surface of your already carved and polychromatic church (for this was the high age of ritual ornament) could be covered, hung, festooned and circled with foliage, crockets, shiny stars, symbolic letters, illuminated crosses, bannerets, devices and brightly coloured texts.

The bustled maidens of the parish and their mutton-chop-bewhiskered beaux would descend on the church in good time before festive Evensong with ladders and nails to fix the artefacts on which they had expended so much labour, love – and expense. Why, a single banner, 36 inches square, illuminated in colours and gold, reading 'Unto us a Child is born, unto us a Son is given', in Gothic script, suitable for hanging between the nave windows, cost 7s 6d. A full price list, from cardboard letters to crystal frost, appeared at the back of the book. The author of *The Art of Garnishing* was Edward Young Cox, and it was published by the firm of Cox & Son (Ecclesiastical Warehouse) of Southampton Street, off the Strand in London. The high technology of chromolithography showed bright examples in green, red and yellow of the lengths to which the garnishers might go.

A church which lacked a reredos or altarpiece at its east end might find itself with one contrived from rods and mesh stuck with everlasting flowers and geometric cut-outs. The style of design is that of the higher denomination Victorian postage stamps – the two-shilling, say – with that somehow solid, quilted, angular and fussy flavour also found on the carved façades of banks or on the cast-iron lids of coal-holes of the time.

According to Mr Cox, any church group of garnishers would need holly, of course, but also *arbor vitae*, Portugal laurel, arbutus, ferns, cypress, rosemary and moss (both real and artificial). They must have rope, stout string, fine twine, reel wire, hoop iron, deal laths, scissors, knives, pliers, bands of perforated zinc and iron clips (for the capitals of columns). The must-haves extended to: cotton velvet, coloured flock papers, imitation silver-paper and paints prepared for use. Most essential was the full range of specially imported gnaphaliums (everlasting flowers) in yellow, white, spotted yellow, crimson, lilac, pink, solferino, black, spotted red, blue, violet, purple and magenta. Victorians liked colour.

Nothing was safe from garnishing. Pillars were spiralled in garlands. The font should acquire 'an iron framework, four to six feet high' to support floral garnishes. A 'very pleasing effect' against the bare walls of the chancel would be diaperings of ornament attached to 'stout iron wire'. The pulpit came in for close attention. The very gas fittings were bravely hung with everlasting flowers.

A new edition of *The Art of Garnishing* came out in 1884, overhauled by Ernest Geldart, with a frontispiece representing the heavily garnished interior of All Saints, Northfleet, Kent, the work of the advanced ritualist architect James Brooks. His chaste, if impressive, interior was transformed.

A new generation came in, influenced by Arts and Crafts simplicity. Christmas evergreens in churches reverted to what children dressed in Kate Greenaway prints were led to believe was the unchanging simplicity of Christmastide, with spare tangles of holly and scarcely a strip of perforated zinc to be seen. Cox & Son published no more catalogues of garnishings.

18 DECEMBER 2004

Up the Flagpole

What flag does your church fly? My local has just replaced its rotting flagstaffs, I am glad to say, and so it was with keen interest that I followed the correspondence in the *Church Times* after a feature on ecclesiastical vexillology – church flag-flying.

According to the Flag Institute, the law in Britain does not govern which flags may be flown. Even so, the Archbishops of Canterbury and York asked the Earl Marshal (the Duke of

Norfolk) in 1938 to issue a warrant indicating that the 'flag proper' to fly from a Church of England church was the Cross of St George with a shield of the arms of the diocese in the top corner nearest the flagpole.

It is only a couple of years since the Cross of St George was won back for respectable use from its kidnappers, the nasty nationalists (tattoos, shaven hair, aggressive dogs). England is not the only country to use it. Georgia, the country not the American state, has now established its national flag as the Cross of St George with, in each quarter, a cross formy (as it's called in heraldry, I think). Barcelona, which also boasts St George as its patron, has got into a fine old mess with its flags, the official flag looking to many people like a logo for some transport company. But the Associacio Catalana de Vexillologia has proposed a flag incorporating the Cross of St George and the four red bars of the Catalan flag.

In comparison, English flag-wearing is a calm backwater. The sort of thing that worries the Flag Institute is a slack halyard, which looks 'very sloppy'. This can be avoided by giving it a couple of turns around the flagpole and tying it as tightly as possible around the cleat. It will also stop noisy clattering, and will save wear on the flag.

The Union flag may also be flown on church towers, according to the Flag Institute. But remember to ensure that the broader white of its St Andrew's Cross is nearest to the top of the flagpole. Otherwise it will be upside-down, a distress sign, as wags will be only too quick to tell.

When it comes to flying flags at half-mast, the Union flag should only be half-masted by royal command, normally as a sign of national mourning. On the death of the monarch, flags should be flown at half-mast until the funeral, except on the day of proclamation of the new monarch. The consensus is that it is improper to fly the Union flag at half-mast for a private funeral. A St George's flag is preferable, unless the dead person has a flag of office or personal banner of arms.

The display of arms, as far as I can make out, is governed by the Court of Chivalry, over which the Earl Marshal presides. The Court of Chivalry had been dormant for some centuries before it was awoken for the case of Manchester Corporation *vs* Manchester

Palace of Varieties in 1954. No doubt European law would affect the Court of Chivalry if it were ever to stir again.

Another official, the Lord Chamberlain, decides when the national flag should be flown on public buildings. He issues advice rather prosaically through the Department of Culture, Media and Sport.

13 MARCH 2004

Abbey Burglar

A burglary in the heart of Westminster Abbey almost robbed us of the remains of Edward the Confessor, whose 1,000th anniversary is being enthusiastically marked this week. It was 1685, and the Abbey was being prepared for the coronation of James II, when a plank or wooden scaffolding pole was dropped, and pierced the coffin of the old king, housed within the nine-foot high tomb that remains to this day. After the coronation, a lay clerk or singing-man named Charles Taylor discovered the hole in the coffin, 'about six inches long and four inches broad'. When he thrust in his arm, his initial discovery scared him. Taylor pulled out an enamelled gold crucifix on a golden chain. 'I was afraid to take them away with me till such time as I had acquainted the Dean,' he wrote later. But in the meantime he inquisitively pulled Edward's head towards the hole in the coffin and found it 'sound and firm, with the upper and nether jaws whole and full of teeth, with a list of gold above an inch broad in the nature of a Coronet surrounding the Temples'.

When Taylor plucked up the courage to tell Dean Sprat of Westminster of his discovery, he was brought before the king himself, who gave orders for the mending and protection of the coffin, but kept the cross. What has become of it I do not know. Perhaps no one does. It was mentioned in the will of Mary of Modena, James's widow, written in 1702.

But the survival of the whole tomb is a stroke of fortune. Most saints' tombs, such as St Thomas Becket's at Canterbury, or St Cuthbert's at Durham, were smashed up at the Reformation. Edward's was spared, no doubt because of his royal status, and only the upper parts were broken up. In Queen Mary's reign a replacement upper tier of wood was added, which is still there.

The stone structure below is pretty, built in the middle of the thirteenth century by Henry III. Some of the work was done by the father-and-son team who constructed the surviving polychromatic pavement (onyx, porphyry, serpentine and coloured glass, with its mysterious Latin inscription) before the high altar of the Abbey. At one corner of Edward's tomb a lovely serpentine column inlaid with brightly coloured mosaic still gives a hint of how splendid the thing must have looked before it was knocked about.

On each side of the tomb are three man-sized niches, used by pilgrims who came to pray there. They would kneel in a niche and offer their prayers to God as near as they could to the saint's holy relics. The Keeper of the Tomb apparently allowed the sick to spend a night lying next to the burial place. It would be interesting to know how often churches were open all night in the Middle Ages; it seems to have been quite often.

As for Edward the Confessor, it is hard to know what happened during his lifetime. We don't even know for certain the year of his birth, but 1005 seems likely. He died in 1066, hence the Battle of Hastings. Of course facts from his reign are known, but the motives behind appointments, depositions, battles, rivalries and the king's manner of life are irrecoverable. Westminster Abbey is his great legacy, although entirely rebuilt two centuries later. When new, in the romanesque style, the wonder of its day, it was unrivalled north of the Alps; an impression is embroidered on the Bayeux tapestry. Edward was canonized in 1161, and the making of a new tomb 100 years later by Henry III (who named his son Edward) became the nucleus for today's funerary clutter in the Abbey.

8 OCTOBER 2005

Wonder of the World

I saw one of the wonders of the world a few days ago. It is a great wall hanging, 13 by 11 feet, depicting the Creation, embroidered in bright colours, and dating from the eleventh century. The tapestry, as people call it (not quite accurately, since it is all sewn, like the Bayeux embroidery), is the prized treasure of Girona Cathedral in Catalonia, for which, perhaps, it was made. The first things to catch the eye are the sea monsters happily sporting in the foreground, in red and green waves helpfully labelled by the embroiderers '*Mare*', the sea.

But in the arched stone room where it hangs, by a subdued light (lest the colours fade), one soon makes out a huge wheel, full of figures occupying segments answering to the six 'days' of creation. In a central roundel sits the youthful-faced Pantocrator, the Ruler of All, his right hand aloft in blessing and in his left an open book inscribed S/CS D/S, '*Sanctus Deus*'. In the corners outside the big wheel, winged figures representing the four winds sit on inflated leather skins. And around the edges are friezes showing the months of the year, the rivers of Paradise, daytime and night and, badly damaged, the discovery of the Holy Cross by St Helena.

The main work within that vast wheel, though, is the focal point. At the top the Holy Spirit, in the form of a haloed dove, hovers over the waters. On one side stands the stern figure of an angel holding a lighted torch, while 'darkness covered the face of the abyss'. (All the captions, embroidered in beautifully formed capital letters, are in Latin.)

On the other side of the Dove stands a cheery angel, with a striped halo, captioned simply '*Lux*'. The designer of the embroidery was aware that light preceded the creation of the sun and moon. But that episode is represented in the neighbouring segment, with God's division of the waters above from the waters below. Their wavy lines are prised open by a greeny-gold circle in which twin smaller circles contain the portraits of the sun (a man with spiky rays beaming from his head and a red-flamed torch in his hand) and the moon (a woman in a coif, bearing a less brightly blazing torch).

Everything is done with energy and delight. Perhaps the quietest segment simply shows dry land emerging from the waves, a disc of vertical stitching amid waves of horizontal stitching. But immediately below the equator of the wheel, life breaks out, with creatures kicking and gambolling.

A ram, goat, cow and horse rear up in front of a hedge where a buck and a unicorn play. Adam stands taking stock, but 'he does not find one like himself' there. So, on the other side of the sea of fishes and monsters – with above them the bright-plumaged '*volatilia caeli*', the birds of heaven – Adam sleeps, and from one of his ribs a woman is formed. Nearby grows the fruit tree, the harbinger of their undoing.

Yet right round the wheel, in a bright silvery rim, is spelled out: 'In the beginning God created heaven and earth and the sea and everything that is in them. And he saw all that he had made, and it was very good.'

It was not that anyone in the eleventh century thought God made everything in six earthly days. (How could he, if the first 'day' had no sun and moon or earth?) St Augustine, whom they read, had written more than 600 years earlier that the six 'days' were logical not historical divisions of the act of creation.

But if this wonderful embroidery does not celebrate the good-ness of creation (against the miserable Manicheans, the body-hating Cathars, the sin-soaked materialists), then I don't know what does. Go and have a look.

30 SEPTEMBER 2006

No Dolls' Eyes

In *The Longest Journey*, E. M. Forster describes the reaction of a visitor to Cambridge coming across the church of Our Lady and the English Martyrs, the first notable building on the way from the railway station: '"Oh, here come the colleges", cries the Protestant parent, and then learns that it was built by a papist who made a fortune out of movable eyes for dolls. "Built with dolls' eyes to house idols" – that at all events is the legend and the joke. It watches the apostate city, taller by many a yard than anything within, and asserting, however wildly, that here is eternity, stability, and bubbles breaking upon a windless sea.'

The true origins and narrow survival of this Victorian pile with its Decorated exuberance, its spire and gargoyles, its tower and steep roofs, are now told in *Catholics in Cambridge*, edited by

Nicholas Rogers (Gracewing). The unlikely benefactor who paid £70,000 for its erection and elaborate furnishing was a ballerina, Pauline Duvernay (1813–94), who had studied under the great Taglioni and Vestris and herself danced at the Paris Opéra and at Drury Lane, where Princess Victoria drew her for her sketch-book.

She married the man reputed to be the richest commoner in England, Stephen Lyne-Stephens, who had not made his money out of dolls' eyes. His death in 1860 left her free to pay for an orphanage and a church or two. The new church in Cambridge, completed in 1890, might have become the Catholic cathedral, had the choice not finally fallen on the equally splendid St John's, Norwich.

The church in Cambridge, designed by the firm of Dunn and Hansom, replaced one built nearby in 1842 by Pugin, modelled on the thirteenth-century St Michael's, Longstanton, Cambridgeshire. Pugin's church was in 1902 dismantled and re-erected at St Ives, Huntingdonshire.

In 1972, a great threat hung over Our Lady and the English Martyrs, with plans to demolish the high altar and baldacchino, put in a raked platform and throw out the pews. A campaign supported by Professor Elizabeth Anscombe, Professor J. A. W. Bennett and Dr David Watkin fended off this disaster.

Mrs Lyne-Stephens' portrait still hangs in the dining-room of the rectory next door, and above the rose window of the church's north transept an inscription in Gothic letters begs prayers for its 'foundress'.

19 JULY 2003

A Secret People

The Daily Telegraph map of Iraq shows in the northern mountains a mysterious people – the Yazidis. They are defined by their religion, but it is not easy to find out what that is. The Yazidis speak Kurdish, an Indo-European language like our own. They live in Iraq, Syria and Turkey, with a few in Armenia. They number 100,000, say some, or 250,000, say others. Ten thousand live in

Germany. Their holy city is Lalish, 50 miles from Mosul, and Jebel Sinjar is their mountain stronghold, although the Iraqi regime deported 20,000 from there in 1975.

They say they are descended from Adam alone, but seem to draw on Zoroastrianism for their beliefs, with a dualistic mythology seeing good and evil as two sides of the cosmos. A central figure is Tawus Melek, one of seven angels made by God. (Muslims often identify him with Eblis, a satanic figure.) He fell into disobedience, repented and spent thousands of years in hell weeping before being rehabilitated. He contains two kinds of fire: good fire as light and bad fire that burns. In the morning Yazidis wash their faces and hands, look to the rising sun and bow three times with arms crossed. They pray thrice daily, keep Wednesdays holy and Saturday as a day of rest.

Yazidis insist on the oral status of their religion, but two holy books have been claimed for them: the *Kitab al-Jelwa* ('The Book of Revelation') and the *Meshaf Resh* ('The Black Book'), copies of which appeared in the West in the late nineteenth century. Their Muslim neighbours suppose from their name that Yazidis honour Yazid, the caliph in 680 to whom Hussein refused to swear allegiance and who is blamed for Hussein's martyrdom. That is a verbal confusion. They are also sometimes taken to be a Shi'a sect. They are mocked for refusing to eat lettuce, in which they say evil is found.

More puzzling is their relationship to Sheikh Adi ibn Musafir, a Sufi mystic who died in AD 1162. They visit his tomb at Lalish in October, sing, dance, play flutes and drums and burn lamps of sesame oil. White bulls are sacrificed. But historians say that the sheikh was a perfectly orthodox Muslim who has had Yazidism thrust on him posthumously. Part of the difficulty here is that of finding out what any unfamiliar religion teaches and practises. (Try explaining Christianity in Britain to a Muslim from abroad.) But Yazidis do seem a strange mix.

10 MAY 2003

Our Own Charterhouse

Surprise is the first emotion that strikes the fortunate visitor to the Charterhouse, on the edge of the City of London, for here, wedged between the traffic fumes of Clerkenwell Road and the bloody pavements of Smithfield meat market, stands a cluster of quadrangles like those of a medieval Oxford college, with hall and chapel, tranquil behind its walls and trees. The ancient buildings are lovely, but there is an air of sadness about the place. The original monastery, dedicated to the 'Salutation' (that is to say, the Annunciation of the Incarnation by the angel Gabriel to the Virgin Mary), was built in the fourteenth century as a monastery for the ascetic Carthusians.

These contemplative monks lived an astonishingly hard life, practically as hermits, each in his tiny house off the cloister, with a garden behind to dig. (A functioning Charterhouse continues today at Parkminster in West Sussex.) The Carthusians, along with the Observant Franciscans of Greenwich and the Bridgettines at Syon, Middlesex, were a spiritual powerhouse for the nation's capital. Befriended by kings when things were going well, they became the first victims of Henry VIII when he fell out with Church authorities.

At the Charterhouse, the quadrangle today called Wash-house Court was built of medieval stonework and completed with a range of brick. The diapering of the brickwork picks out the initials JH, those of John Houghton, the prior from 1531 to 1535. In the latter year, he refused to swear an oath recognizing Henry VIII as supreme head of the Church, and he was hanged, drawn and quartered at Tyburn on 4 May.

One of his arms was nailed to the door of the Charterhouse, but this did not dissuade 15 of his brother Carthusians from holding out. Five died on the scaffold and the other ten were starved to death in Newgate prison.

Even after the Charterhouse was re-endowed in 1611 by the legacy of Thomas Sutton, the landowner and moneylender, to give lodging to poor old men and education to boys, the uncomfortable memory remained that the buildings had once been inhabited by better men. When the future novelist Thackeray arrived at the school in 1821, aged ten, he found it dominated by flogging and fagging. He said he was 'abused into sulkiness' and 'bullied into despair', and later depicted the school under the name Slaughterhouse. There was nothing out of the ordinary about this among the public schools of the time and Charterhouse School changed completely with its move to Godalming in 1872.

The remaining foundation of Sutton's Hospital, smashed and burnt in part by the Blitz, but restored, still looks after 40 old men and does it very well, what with the expense of compliance with health and safety rules and the modern expectations of extended medical care for old people. But, in the middle of the twentieth century, something happened that addressed the discomfort of its historical inheritance.

Geoffrey Curtis (1902–81) was a member of the Anglican religious Community of the Resurrection, at Mirfield in West Yorkshire. In 1938, he edited a contemporary account of the martyrdom of the Carthusians and began to campaign for a memorial plaque to them at the London Charterhouse. He hoped to transform an atmosphere that 'chills so mortally the relations between the established church and the church of Rome in England'. Deaths, war and finances delayed his ambition, but he persevered until, in 1958, in the open air at the site of the high altar of the former priory church, a plaque was set up.

'Remember before God,' it says, 'the monks and lay-brothers of the Carthusian house of the Salutation who worshipped at this altar and for conscience sake endured torment and death.' And now, the 25th anniversary of Geoffrey Curtis's death, a neat plaque to his memory has been fixed on the wall of the ante-chapel of the Charterhouse. A requiem Eucharist was sung and the Archbishop of Canterbury, himself once a lecturer at Mirfield, sent a message calling Curtis 'a servant of the unity of God's Church and a man whose prayerful quiet gave him a true insight into the Carthusian martyrs, whose witness he chronicled'.

Charterhouse is a microcosm of England: historic, battered, torn by ideologies, modest and beautiful. The scandal of Christian disunity cannot be addressed without awareness of its historical roots. The initiative at the Charterhouse to honour the work begun by Geoffrey Curtis is a generous and brave one.

13 MAY 2006

Letters on the Wall

I wrote here last month that some diapering on early Tudor brick-work at the Charterhouse in London spelt out the initials of John Houghton, its prior up to 1535, the year he was martyred. Two people whose opinions I respect have said I am wrong, and that those initials JH or IH stand not for Houghton's name, but are the remnants of the monogram IHS, standing for the name of Jesus.

This is likely. It is argued that as a good Carthusian, Houghton would not have perpetuated his own name on the building. Other religious men might do otherwise, as we find at St Bartholomew the Great in London. There the stonework is carved with a barrel pierced by a crossbow shaft – making the rebus or name-play of 'bolt-tun' after Abbot William Bolton (who died in 1532). But Bolton, who oversaw the construction of Henry VII's chapel at Westminster Abbey, was better known as a builder than a spiritual leader.

Another builder was John Alcock (1430–1500), Bishop of Ely, where his rebus, a cock standing on a globe, is to be seen in stone and glass. Though a cleric, he was not a member of a religious order; and though a builder, he was not a worldly man, having several of his books on the spiritual life (including *The Hill of Perfection*) printed by Caxton's colleague Wynkyn de Worde.

But in an age of exuberant heraldry, the badge of the Carthusians remained simply a cross on an orb with seven stars, representing their founder St Bruno and his first six companions, who entered the 'desert' of the valley of Chartreuse in 1084. Their motto is '*Stat crux dum volvitur orbis*', 'Stands the Cross, still point of the turning world'.

The Carthusian vocation is a hermit's life, silent and anonymous 'in the face of God'. These monks leave their cells only to pray in the monastery church or to eat a meatless meal in silence with their brethren on feast days. One day that they observe as a feast is that on which a fellow Carthusian is buried, in a walled burial ground, with no coffin, beneath a wooden cross that bears no name. In this context, the picking out of a Carthusian prior's initials in brickwork is hardly convincing. What, then, of the monogram IHS?

The name of Jesus in early Greek manuscripts of the New

Testament was often abbreviated to the first and last letters – *iota* and *sigma*, written as IC. Sometimes the second letter of the name was included too – an *eta*, which, as a capital, looked like our letter H. The terminal form of the letter *sigma* often appeared more like the Roman letter S, hence IHS.

In the fourth century, even in Latin, the name Jesus continued to be written IHS. In later centuries the letters were reinterpreted as standing for '*Iesus Hominum Salvator*', 'Jesus, the Saviour of Mankind'. The fifteenth century saw a growth in devotion to the name of Jesus, popularized by Bernardine of Siena. When preaching, he used as a visual aid 'IHS' written in letters of gold within a roundel. At first, he got into trouble for encouraging superstition. This might sound odd in a post-Reformation world, where depiction of saints seems more open to superstition than a written word. But the worry in the fifteenth century was that the monogram IHS might be regarded as a talisman.

Bernardine's intentions were quite otherwise. He not only wanted to stop the taking of the Lord's name in vain, but wanted reverence for the name to develop into love for the person whose name it is. The Pope was convinced, and Bernardine's preaching flourished. He was declared a saint in 1455.

Devotion to the name of Jesus would have been very familiar to John Houghton. His house was dedicated to the Annunciation. In the Church's calendar, that is not a feast of the Virgin Mary, but a feast of the Lord. Whose initials could better stand on the walls that St John Houghton had built?

3 JUNE 2006

Cope Jealousy

A strange lawsuit has been brought by a 13-year-old choirgirl against the Dean and Chapter of Lincoln. She claims damages for the 'mental anguish' she says she suffered by not being awarded the right to wear a 'cope' during choir processions. Whatever the poor girl's feelings, readers have been much entertained by the absurdities of the case. Meanwhile, I was moved to wonder why choirgirls should wear copes in the first place.

A cope is usually thought of as a liturgical vestment, for use by a bishop or priest in church. The Rt Rev. Richard Chartres, the Bishop of London, wore a heavy black and gold cope at the service at St Paul's for the anniversary of the outrage in New York on 11 September. The other day, I saw a clergyman standing at the wicket gate of the porter's lodge of Exeter College, Oxford, waiting for a wedding party to arrive. Those are the sort of circumstances in which copes make an appearance.

A cope laid flat makes a big semicircle. You can see wooden cope-chests of that shape in some cathedrals and old collegiate churches. These helped preserve copes for hundreds of years. There is a wonderful example, called the Syon cope, at the Victoria and Albert Museum, which dates from the thirteenth century and depicts men and angels in gold and silver thread with the kind of embroidery celebrated in its day as *opus anglicanum.* In origin, copes are reckoned, like chasubles, to have been, in ancient times, ordinary items of wear for secular use. Fine ones, Sunday best, were dedicated by their owners to use during church services. As far as the English word goes, it is a variant of cape. In the sixteenth century, translators of ancient Latin works used cope to render the word toga. In design, the essential difference between a cope and a chasuble is that the cope was not sewn up at the front; it was an open cloak.

The survival of the cope in the Church of England was something of a fluke at the Reformation. Copes are sanctioned for use by bishops and priests during the administration of Communion in a rubric to the first Prayer Book of Edward VI. But the chasuble fell by the wayside during the tussles of the Elizabethan settlement, while the cope survived. None of this helped me understand why a schoolgirl should want to wear a cope. What I hadn't realized is that, in parallel with the priestly cope, another item of clothing with the same name developed. This was the choir-cope or *cappa choralis.* It was worn by monks or collegiate clergy during the singing of the Divine Office, which is to say, the psalms arranged for recitation at intervals from matins to compline.

The cope worn in choir was also used by the Dominican and Franciscan friars for winter warmth. Chaucer refers to the copes of friars. This kind of cope is generally of a woollen cloth, and usually black, as with the choirgirls' copes of Lincoln. A picture of one worn by a choirboy is available on Lincoln Cathedral's website. As it happens, the website doesn't show a girl wearing one.

14 SEPTEMBER 2002

Lucky Strike

On the morning of Friday 15 July 1927, workmen were digging a cellar for a shop on the new road to the station at Douai in northern France when a pick found a leaden coffin five feet below the surface. Thinking it might be buried treasure, one man was all for breaking it open on the spot. Fortunately, he was dissuaded. The mayor and the police were called in and that weekend the press became excited by prospects of Douai's 'own Tutankhamun' (whose tomb had been discovered five years earlier).

That Saturday, a workman threw away something like a bit of old carpet. It later turned out to have been the hair shirt of Thomas Becket, preserved since 1170. When the lead coffin was eased open, it contained a man's body with some peculiar injuries to it. The head was sewn on to the body. The hands were missing but the skin of the face was 'of a coppery colour and there was a slight moustache and beard à la Richelieu'. Albert Purdie, an Englishman summoned to France by someone on the spot who knew he might have the key to the mystery, was pretty sure the body was that of a holy man hurriedly buried in the precincts of the English College, Douay (as they spelled it), during the French Revolution.

The revolutionaries not only sought reliquaries for the value of their precious metals but also took pains to smash and scatter sacred remains of the old religion of France – as happened at the royal burial church of St Denis and a thousand other sites. Purdie suspected that the body belonged to John Southworth, a London priest executed in Cromwell's day. He was known to have been buried with honour in the chapel of the English College, Douay. Moreover, Purdie knew that Fr Thomas Stout, the General

35

Prefect of the College in 1793, had drawn a plan of where 'relics' and the saintly Southworth's body were hidden in the Revolution. But the plan had gone missing.

Two months after the discovery of the body, a copy of Stout's plan was found in the archives of Douai Abbey, Woolhampton, Berks. The plans showed an outhouse of the English College, Douay, with an X for the 'relics' (including Becket's shirt) and a dotted line marking John Southworth's burial place. Any doubt about the identity of the remains was settled.

John Southworth was declared a saint in 1970. His life had been blameless, as he went around bravely visiting those caught in the frequent outbreaks of plague that preceded the great epidemic of 1665. Sometimes healthy people were locked up in infected houses and had no one to fetch food or attend to them spiritually. John Southworth's own death was of a piece with his life. He had been arrested at the instigation of a bounty-hunting informer but clearly the judge before whom he was brought was reluctant to condemn him.

'When the old man [he was 62] would not be drawn to deny himself to be a priest,' says an old account, 'the magistrate was so drowned in tears upon the sad occasion that it was long before he could pronounce the sentence.' Southworth was hanged, drawn and quartered at Tyburn, where Marble Arch is now. 'The Lord Protector lately fought long for the liberty of the subject,' he said in his speech on the scaffold, 'and the people of this nation were made believe there should be a general liberty of conscience and that no man's life should be taken away for matters of religion, for which only I die.'

His body lies in a glass case in a chapel at Westminster Cathedral, dressed in ancient vestments. He is the only Roman Catholic martyr of those days whose body has been saved from a common grave or worse, thanks to the ingenuity of the collegians of 1793 and a lucky pick-strike in 1927.

19 JUNE 2004

Cathedral Charges

English cathedrals have started reimposing admission charges or introducing more or less compulsory 'donations'. Their finances are under strain because fewer foreign tourists have been bringing in money since 11 September 2001. But the reappearance of the turnstile is 'bound to create disquiet and raise some fundamental questions about the nature of the cathedrals' future work'. That is the opinion of the Very Rev. Trevor Beeson, whose new book is called *The Deans* (SCM Press). He speaks from experience, for he spent a decade as Dean of Winchester.

It is the deans who run cathedrals, with the cathedral chapter, and local bishops have less say over them than over any other church in their dioceses. Trevor Beeson does not use the word 'betrayal' of the imposition of entry charges, but he does say that the abolition of such obstacles to entry is 'essential to a cathedral's mission'. It is only 80 years since cathedrals were opened up without payment to visitors and worshippers, and the man who made it possible is one of Trevor Beeson's heroes, Frank Bennett, who transformed Chester Cathedral in the 1920s.

Bennett did not want to be Dean of Chester when he was appointed in 1920. He had had little contact with cathedrals and 'looked upon deans as the fortunate occupants of an office in the Church of England that could easily be dispensed with altogether'. But by 1925, when he published *The Nature of a Cathedral*, he had not only changed his ideas, he had established a working model of a cathedral as 'the Bishop's and his family's great House of Prayer'. By 'family' Bennett meant principally the people of the diocese, and he saw as 'outrageous' the charging of sixpence for those people 'to whom the cathedral really belongs', to spend a limited time looking round it.

That was the usual thing. Vergers could act almost as showmen. In the nineteenth century, Westminster Abbey had waxworks exhibited for the paying customer. Frank Bennett threw open the doors of Chester Cathedral from early morning to dusk. Beautifully printed and framed notices explained the purpose of various parts of the building. Side chapels were looked after by diocesan organizations – the Mothers' Union, the Scouts and so on.

There were no locked gates and no officials demanding six-pence. Voluntary donations outdid former fees fourfold. Dean Bennett abolished the singing of early-morning matins, preferring to concentrate on sung evensong, choosing popular items of music when larger congregations gathered on Saturdays. The daily services were: matins (said, not sung) at 7.30 a.m.; Eucharist at 7.50 a.m. (said, but sung on Wednesday and Friday at 9.15 a.m.); sung evensong at 5 p.m. A far-reaching innovation was 'people's Communion' at 9 a.m. on Sundays.

In most parishes at the time the lengthy programme of Sunday services was enough to 'fairly wear the godly out and frighten the not very godly clean away'. A 9 a.m. Communion, with organ and singing, was not as daunting as an earlier service, for working people who had spent the week getting up early, and it gave families free time after its conclusion at about 10 a.m. For him, tinkering with service times was not the whole answer. If the cathedral was to be the great House of Prayer for the bishop and his 'family', then he had to live near the cathedral and enter into its life regularly. Bennett rebuilt the ruined monastic refectory at Chester not just as a commercial teashop, but to serve the parties from all over the diocese who came to use the cathedral. Parish groups would hold short services in the cathedral and end their visit with lunch or tea in the refectory.

Since Bennett's day, ordinary life has become less integrated with the parish church. But interest in cathedrals remains high. BBC2 has just begun a new prime-time series on their history. In Trevor Beeson's view, the realization that mission is the priority in Christian life means that the parish system will be remade. Meanwhile cathedrals must retain their 'heritage' role, provide theological resources for the diocese, and, foremost, ensure that worship of the highest level is offered.

8 JANUARY 2005

3

Inside Books

Mma Ramotswe's Morals

Precious Ramotswe is a lady of traditional build living on the outskirts of Gaborone. She enjoys a mug of bush tea as the sun grows hotter in the morning, and a large slice of fruit cake when offered one by Mma Potokwani, who so admirably runs the Orphan Farm. Mma Ramotswe is the heroine of six novels by Alexander McCall Smith, beginning with *The No. 1 Ladies' Detective Agency*. The books have become immensely popular thanks to word-of-mouth recommendation.

As she drives her tiny white van on her detective missions, Mma Ramotswe has time to think of the old Botswana. She is grateful to the late Sir Seretse Khama, a good man who made Botswana a good place. But things are changing. 'People did not seem to understand the difference between right and wrong,' she muses. 'If you left it to them to work out for themselves, they would never bother. They would just find out what was best for them, and then they would call that the right thing.' 'Most morality', she thinks at one point in the third book, *Morality for Beautiful Girls*, 'was about doing the right thing because it had been identified as such by a long process of acceptance and observation.'

For Mma Ramotswe, morality is exercised in a community and passed down. It is connected to traditional manners. She is a stickler for enquiring on meeting someone, even a stranger, how they have slept. She dislikes the new, westernized habit of taking a gift with one hand, instead of extending both politely. She notices in an old photograph that 'everybody was looking at the camera with courtesy, with an attitude of moral attention. That was the old Botswana way'. It was of a piece with picking up a hat that someone has lost and putting it in a safe place – on top of a wall, say – to be found.

In Botswana, Mma Ramotswe notes, the attitude is taken as far as calling anyone, a stranger or traveller, 'brother' or 'sister'. She reads of anthropologists positing the origin of all mankind in East Africa; so the convention of sisterhood might, she muses, have a scientific basis. As William Lancaster has pointed out in his work on Bedouin, which Mma Ramotswe seems not yet to have read, obligations between cousins extend ever outward; ultimately all human beings, Arab or not, are children of Adam.

In *The Kalahari Typing School for Men*, the fourth book, she considers the impenetrable Botswana penal code. 'She wondered whether it might not be simpler to rely on something like the Ten Commandments, which, with a bit of modernisation, seemed to be a perfectly good set of guidelines for the conduct of one's life.'

Yet morality is more than the application of a set of rules. In Mma Ramotswe's world some people are good, starting with her late Daddy. He not only brought up this motherless girl with care, but treated her as a moral agent with innate dignity. When her no-good husband Note Mokoti beat her and abandoned her with a dead baby, she returned to her Daddy. He did not speak a word of reproach for her ill-judged marriage. Her friend Mr J. L. B. Matekoni is a good man too, and she is a good woman. She gives a woman a job as a maid because she sees the woman's child waiting outside the yard, standing on one toe for luck. If her mother got the job there might be supper that night.

Even more remarkable is the theme of *The Kalahari Typing School for Men*: reparation. A man asks the detective agency to trace two people he has wronged years before. Mma Ramotswe makes sure he does not just pay them off, but makes contact and helps them. 'I could never be a judge,' she thinks. 'I could not sit there and punish people after they have begun to feel sorry.'

Alexander McCall Smith is a professor of medical law at Edinburgh. He was the first chairman of the ethics committee of the *British Medical Journal*. Medical ethics are the devil – very practical and very difficult.

I do not want to make the novels sound pious or soppy. They are not. But they have an impressively humane, moral dimension.

14 AUGUST 2004

Ulfire and Jale

A Voyage to Arcturus has been a cult book since its publication in 1920. That means most people do not get round to reading it. In the lifetime of its author, David Lindsay (1876–1945), it sold fewer than 600 copies. It has been called 'one of the greatest books of the century', but that was by Colin Wilson, the author of *The Outsider.*

The book – better than science fiction – undoubtedly had a huge influence on C. S. Lewis, most obviously on his two inter-planetary books, *Out of the Silent Planet* and *Perelandra* (retitled, by a dim publisher eager for a wider market, *Voyage to Venus*). *Arcturus* goes further than Philip Pullman, and Lewis was fascin-ated by it partly because it seemed nearly diabolical.

Lindsay's book is a *tour de force* of other-worldly imagination. On a planet orbiting Arcturus and its twin star, people with alien sense organs live among pinnacles of rock that shoot up or fall away without warning, under the unbearable noon of Blodsom-bre and the emotionally torturing light of the second sun Alppain. The desert may be bright red, the snow green, but airborne plants reveal new colours, ulfire and jale.

As it happens I think that the philosophical content of *Arc-turus*, which is unconvincing in itself, best serves to reinforce its imaginative weirdness. What I mean is that the theories Lindsay deploys are neither original nor coherent. He has a sort of Gnostic or, more obviously, Manichaean view of creation. He puts sex, along with beauty, as the work of the evil one, and reduces redemptive sacrifice to mere pain. It is unusual to discuss such ideas at all in a work of fiction, but by turning the delight of beauty, goodness, love and existence upside down as effects of evil, Lindsay wraps his other world in a nightmarish quality that gives it a disturbing impact.

Nor do I think Lindsay knew entirely what he was doing. Every-one agrees that he doesn't write well technically. Yet his book cannot be left to one side once begun, even though its plot is no more than a mysterious journey during which ten strange char-acters appear and declaim, often provoking another killing by the hero Maskull.

C. S. Lewis produced a sort of fictional antidote to Lindsay in his own interplanetary books. *Perelandra* is his version of a satanic assault on a newly peopled planet. In a way it tells the same story as *A Voyage to Arcturus*, but in a cosmos made by a beneficent deity, where Lindsay had suggested that beauty and joy were the work of an evil demiurge. And yet Lewis had more in common with Lindsay than his image as a Christian apologist at first suggests.

Lewis's first volume of poetry, *Spirits in Bondage* (1918), was based on the idea that 'nature is wholly diabolical and malevolent and that God, if He exists, is outside and opposite of the cosmic arrangement'. Even after decades as a Christian, in his bereavement Lewis was haunted by the fear that the universe was run by a sadistic god. As a teenager, Lewis had had a double fascination with sadism and with the Prometheus myth of a hero pitted against the gods. In *Arcturus* both elements are evident.

In 1938, three years after reading *A Voyage to Arcturus*, Lewis wrote an unfinished story called *The Dark Tower*. In the tower of the title a man sits with a sting projecting from his forehead. *Arcturus* begins and ends with a dark tower, and the hero's forehead is constantly modified by new organs. Perhaps Lewis left his story unfinished because it was too derivative.

Yet Lewis did not need Lindsay's invention to feed his imagination. He found the pre-Copernican cosmos stimulating enough, as he shows in *The Discarded Image*. And many years before reading *Arcturus*, Lewis had, in Norse tales and in such benign myth as George MacDonald's *Phantastes*, grasped hold of 'joy', the experience he sought and that Lindsay attacked.

David Lindsay has gained a short entry in the new *Dictionary of National Biography*. He was a failed writer and a miserable man, but he provokes ideas in his readers, for the only reading of *Arcturus* that is good enough is one that argues back.

12 MARCH 2005

Brilliant Pages

The Lindisfarne Gospels are simply breathtaking. The very gold and brilliance of their pages suggest there was quite a lot of light in the Dark Ages. And culturally there is nothing insular about this high achievement of the Insular school of calligraphy. A new book by Michelle P. Brown, which links this codex of 259 vellum folios with the world of the great scholar Bede (670–735), also rethinks what the written word meant to the Anglo-Saxons.

It is a commonplace to assert that the scriptural word assumed importance after the coming of printing and the Reformation. Dr Brown in *The Lindisfarne Gospels* (British Library) demonstrates the religious reverence with which the words of Scripture were regarded in pre-Conquest England. Bede himself describes the reading of the Gospel as *ruminatio*. In Cicero's time *ruminatio* had already meant, as well as chewing the cud, a mental turning over of things. For Bede, it was meditation or contemplation.

Nor did it escape the Anglo-Saxon mind that the Gospel is the word of God, and in St John's Gospel the 'Word' is a name for Jesus. Jesus is also called Immanuel, 'God with us', and the word of the Gospel is God's word with us.

For the monks who made the Lindisfarne Gospels, followers of the spirituality of St Cuthbert, the book of the Gospel was like the Ark of the Covenant in which God was present to the people of Israel. It was the duty of the monk to enter in spirit the holy place of the Ark and to transmit the word, through writing, to future generations.

The text of the Lindisfarne Gospels is a very accurate, beautifully written version of the Latin translation made by St Jerome, known as the Vulgate. This was universally regarded as a masterpiece that faithfully passed on the meaning of the Greek originals. Indeed the translators of the English version of 1611 often leant on the Vulgate themselves. (In the tenth century, someone wrote an earlier English rendering between the lines of the Lindisfarne Gospels.)

Dr Brown thinks that the Lindisfarne Gospels were made in about 715 to mark a new unity of practice between the Anglo-Saxon and Celtic traditions. They were a triumph of hope, and they have survived.

30 AUGUST 2003

Wesley's *Imitation*

'Notwithstanding his night-labours, both in transcribing the Bible and writing out his own meditations, he never used spectacles.' So wrote John Wesley of Thomas à Kempis (1380–1471), who died in his 92nd year. It is the sort of thing he would have noted. We celebrate next Tuesday the 300th anniversary of Wesley's birth. What a volcano he was! He lived to 88, having 'first begun to feel old at 85' and complaining of bad eyesight in his last year. So many miles walked or ridden (225,000), so many sermons preached (40,000), such a singleness of mind.

But it is à Kempis's *Imitation of Christ* that I want to touch on now. Wesley translated the classic in 1735, three years before he underwent an experience of conversion, but a decade after his first commitment to a regular, methodical life of piety. In 1777, on laying the foundation stone for the new chapel in City Road, he looked back: 'In 1725 a young student at Oxford was much affected by reading Kempis . . .' It was in his luggage when he went out a missionary to America. In 1782, he named it among the few books a Methodist Circuit should not lack. He directed that the Methodist school at Kingswood should study it in Latin – not à Kempis's original, but in a more Ciceronian renaissance rendition.

There are greater similarities between Wesley and à Kempis, the fifteenth-century Augustinian monk, than might seem likely. 'He never declined it, when desired to speak upon an improving subject,' Wesley says of à Kempis, 'only desiring a little time to prepare himself for it by meditation. And the ease and eloquence with which he spoke were so great, that many came from remote places to hear him.'

The kernel of *The Imitation* – to let Jesus into the heart – was felt by Wesley strongly. And then, as Wesley notes in his preface, 'the chief instruments or means of Christian life are, above all and in all, the grace of God, and in subserviency to this, prayer, self-examination, reading the scriptures and the holy communion'.

The tragedy of Wesley's life seemed to be the Methodist Connexion falling out of unity with the Church of England (of which Wesley was a priest all his days). Since then, Methodism has had its effects on other nonconformist Christians. The recognition of à Kempis's value by Wesley connects Christians from far wider traditions than find it easy to be on close terms.

31 May 2003

Love's Laundry

Rowan Williams, the Archbishop of Canterbury, was, if anything, too kind to the press in a lecture he gave the other day. The media, he said, 'promises to deliver what other sources can't, information that is needed to equip the reader or viewer or listener for a more free and significant role as a human agent. But at the same time, it is bound to a method and a rhetoric that treats its public as consumers and the information it purveys as a commodity'.

Judging by things that Dr Williams has said before about turning people into mere consumers whose freedom is subverted, newspapers are doing the work of Satan. And all the thanks Dr Williams got for pointing this out was a slightly unfair comment that he uses language that is too obscure to get through to the public with the success that the press thinks it enjoys. Still, Dr Williams's previous assertion that, in 'apophatic' theology, 'we must let go of the control of conceptual analysis' is doubtless true, but not much help to those not familiar with the shady walks of apophatic theology.

This strain of theology is all about denying that God is limited by our little human pigeon-holes. Most people are happy saying, 'God is not finite'. It is not so obvious that there is truth in saying, 'God is not good'. For that to be a reasonable thing to say, one has to add riders, explaining that God is not just as good as a human being conceives goodness, but is better. He is certainly not bad.

Knowledge of God beyond plain reasoning forms part of what is known as 'mysticism'. Mysticism is, to be sure, susceptible to abuse. Foolish people speak of things 'beyond good and evil'. Others mistake dimness of intellect for transcendence of it. England has been strong on mystical prayer. The fourteenth century saw a succession of confident writers: Julian of Norwich and Walter Hilton and the anonymous author of *The Cloud of Unknowing*, a fearless pilot of the apophatic twilight. Dr Williams is very familiar with these writers, and with their sixteenth-century successors, the Welshman Augustine Baker and the Spaniards Teresa of Avila and John of the Cross.

Dr Williams is, like John of the Cross, a poet. Although I hate the fallacy of thinking that prayer is merely another way of saying what poetry says, poetry can say things that cannot be said in less metaphorical terms. In that way it is a little like liturgy.

I've just been reading *The Poems of Rowan Williams* (The Perpetua Press), a 90-page collection. Some are on nature, some on death. Others reflect on icons ('Our Lady of Vladimir' or 'Rublev's Trinity'). The poems are far from sloppy; black is a common word. Here is a short poem on a chapel at the church of the Holy Sepulchre in Jerusalem. It is called 'Calvary'.

> The metalled O. Like Bethlehem, like
> a baroque drain in the marble floor;
> when your hand has been sucked in, it comes away
> from its complicity moist,
> grimy, sweet-scented.

I don't know why 'complicity', but I have seen the metalled O at Bethlehem, with its inscription, *Hic verbum caro factum est*. If you like Rowan Williams's poems, you might like those of the historian and translator Pauline Matarasso, whose volume *The Price of Admission* has just been published by Broughton House Books. Rowan Williams has a poem on Gwen John as Mrs Noah, too long to quote here. Pauline Matarasso has a short poem on a sentence from *The Cloud of Unknowing* ('And therefore she hung up her love and her longing desire in this cloud of unknowing' – Chapter 16):

> Reaching her arms so high
> she thrust them through
> to peg love's laundry in the sky
> and white against the blue
> her banners flew.

25 JUNE 2005

The Suicide Club

Anyone who has read *Kidnapped* knows that Robert Louis Stevenson was a marvellously powerful storyteller as well as a great stylist. Less well known is his early story *The Suicide Club*, first published in periodical form when he was still in his twenties. It is extraordinary, not for its storytelling power, since the plot is implausible, but for conveying a feeling of joy in living. It immediately reminded me of G. K. Chesterton. Chesterton was born in 1874, 24 years after Stevenson, and was a great admirer of his. He never acquired Stevenson's compelling narrative skill, but he shared, if not derivatively, the same sort of existential wonder, as outlined in his novel *Manalive*, and most memorably expressed in *The Man Who Was Thursday*.

That novel begins with a breakfast for a club of murderous anarchists on a balcony on full view in Leicester Square. Stevenson's *The Suicide Club* begins in the pubs around Leicester Square, where (for no reason of the author's, apart from an interest in strangeness), a young man is described attempting to give away cream tarts. Stevenson had a strong element of contrariness in his nature. He adhered to no religious creed, but in his last years assumed the outward forms of Christianity among the people of Samoa. Amid the careful Calvinism of his parents' people in Scotland he fought free from convention; among the Pacific islanders he taught in Sunday school and composed prayers for his household. He embraced energetically a moral code which did not coincide with the conventions of British life in the second half of the nineteenth century, and in particular he admired the French trait of a 'universal indulgence towards all sexual problems', according to his stepson, Lloyd Osbourne.

At the same time Stevenson hated materialism. 'He judged it to be the supreme danger and curse of our civilization,' Osbourne judged – 'that comfortable, well-fed, complacent materialism against which he was always railing.' He was certain that the life after death was something to look forward to. Though he spent the second half of his 44 years on earth in the hourly expectation of a lung haemorrhage that might kill him, that did not prevent him toying with the idea of jumping the gun.

To reach the desirable other country, 'Why shrink from using the equivalent of a railway ticket?' he once asked a group of listeners, by his wife's account. 'Just a few pennies' worth of prussic acid. How exhilarating for several friends – say the present party – to make the journey in company, and hand in hand embark on a journey that would end in paradise!' From this idea grew his story *The Suicide Club*, but the story has quite a different flavour from the cheerful contrariness of his conversational proposal. The fictional club achieves suicide by a method of vicarious murder. And the victim, once chosen by the turn of a playing-card, doesn't necessarily want to go. Stevenson shrewdly makes the members of the club mostly 'people in the prime of youth, with every show of intelligence and sensibility in their appearance, but with little promise of strength or the quality that makes success'. Not a few were still in their teens.

The young man with the cream tarts joins the club, but learns to hate its aims. The remainder of the tale is concerned with the hunting down of the club's murderous president, who has made himself rich on other men's desperation.

In real life, Stevenson was an invalid but no valetudinarian. He wore his hair long lest a haircut bring on a cold that could provoke a fatal haemorrhage, but he would not make himself comfortable in carpet slippers. 'I want to die with my boots on,' he would say. But once in Samoa, he went barefoot indoors like everyone else, and in that warm climate he had his hair cut. Here he chose a way of life the opposite to that of the Suicide Club, and here he was to die.

29 APRIL 2006

Cherie on GKC

Cherie Booth, the wife of the Prime Minister, made quite a good joke last week during a surprise visit to the Athenaeum club in London. 'The whole world is dividing itself into progressives and conservatives,' she said. 'The job of the progressives is to go on making mistakes. The job of the conservatives is to prevent those mistakes from being corrected.'

As she readily acknowledged, the joke was lifted from G. K. Chesterton, for he was the motive for her being there, at a meeting to raise funds for the Chesterton Institute, based in Oxford and New Jersey. Americans are good at raising funds, but we British seem hopeless at it and, unless people rally round, the Chesterton Institute, with its library in Oxford that spreads his ideas, will founder.

That matters, because it was not after all so unlikely that Miss Booth should be a fan of Chesterton's. What he says continues to be valued across a wide spectrum of political views. Chesterton was politically a Liberal, a supporter of the Boers during the Boer War, an excoriator of capitalism, a defender of the French Revolution, an admirer of the anomalous Robert Browning and G. F. Watts. He moved towards Catholicism at a time when it was surprising the world with its radical social doctrine.

He is still enjoyed not as a mere ideologue. His prose style may be relentlessly paradoxical on the surface, but beneath it are great sinews of original thought. And when he is not original he is presenting old ideas afresh, just as he suggests, in *Orthodoxy* (1908), that a man might rediscover England as if it were a strange South Sea island. Indeed his striking talent was to see the world through new eyes, as a Manalive (the title of one of his novels of ideas). Certainly his vision grew into one of a Christianity that transforms reality. The glazing bars of a window for him were in the shape of the Cross. But his was not a stodgy, roast-beef English religion, nor yet a toast-and-water piosity. His short book on Thomas Aquinas presents the theologian not as a dry schoolman but as a sort of existential rationalist, where 'rationalist' means someone who uses reason to bring home the reality of the world made by God.

If some of Chesterton's contemporary Christian philosophers were methodic realists, eschewing the acrid fog of Germanic idealism, Chesterton was a methodic optimist.

He was a child of Victorian scepticism and pessimism, left to grow up on the sterile shingle landscape of Matthew Arnold's 'Dover Beach', dominated by the 'melancholy, long, withdrawing roar' of the sea of faith. Chesterton was to produce his own memorably dour lines, 'I tell you naught for your comfort,/Yea, naught for your desire,/Save that the sky grows darker yet/And the sea rises higher.' But these are set in the context of a heroism that is Christian, ultimately hopeful, not nihilistic.

Chesterton had taken an overdose of nihilism in the 1890s when he was at the Slade School of Art. It was an intellectual world, 'where the perverse in pleasure pine/And men are weary of green wine/And sick of crimson seas', to take some more lines from 'The Ballad of the White Horse'. Beneath the black moon of the French symbolists and the deceiving planchette of the spiritualists, Chesterton found sulphur and blackness. He only escaped by grasping tight to the shafts of light that entered this black hole.

Miss Booth did not go into all this during her short speech last week, and might not agree with it for all I know. But she did praise the impressive periodical the *Chesterton Review*, which is celebrating its 30th anniversary under the editorship of its founder, the remarkable Fr Ian Boyd. It had tried to promote 'a benign cultural revolution', Miss Booth said, 'and a revival of interest in intelligent Christianity – meaning a Christianity that is traditional without being fundamentalist, and radical without being aggressive'.

22 OCTOBER 2005

4

Talking with God

Prayers that Work

I have been busy compiling an anthology of prayers. The question is whether people will find them of any use. I hoped that they would, so much so that I thought of calling the book *Prayers that Work*. But I could see the absurdity of that, implying as it might that no other prayers work.

In fact you cannot tell someone else how to pray. Christians are familiar with the insight of St Paul: 'We know not what we should pray for as we ought, but the Spirit itself maketh intercession for us with groanings which cannot be uttered.' Everyone has this personal tutor, even if they are not explicitly aware of his actions. It is precisely the unutterableness of these promptings that leaves verbal formulations looking feeble.

But what I was getting at in the rejected title, *Prayers that Work*, was indeed that prayers are only any use if they are made one's own. The wicked Claudius in *Hamlet* kneels on stage (while Hamlet is wondering whether to stab him then and there), and after a bit gets up, saying, 'My words fly up, my thoughts remain below./Words without thoughts never to heaven go.' In order to 'work', prayers have to come out from our minds somehow. Yet if we know prayers off by heart we find that it is hard to pay attention to them when we say them. Even so, I think that prayers known by heart can 'work' in four ways.

1. They can be said straightforwardly, aloud or to ourselves, and mean just what they say. One can say the Lord's Prayer, the 'Our Father', like that, although, if one is at the same time monitoring whether one is paying attention, it is 100 to one against getting to the end with much awareness of what each petition said.

2. Familiar prayers can be made to work by using them as prompts during a period of mental prayer. All I mean by 'mental

prayer' is the few minutes that a lot of people like to set aside when they can be alone with God, considering his presence and conversing, as it were, mentally. But sometimes nothing comes to mind, or what comes to mind has nothing much to do with God. So a phrase from a well-known prayer can pull thoughts back to God. Classic writers on prayer often liken such short prayers to kindling to get a fire going.

3. Paradoxically, formulas of prayer can be used by not paying attention to their words. That might sound shocking. But, in the Eastern Christian tradition, the 'Jesus prayer' is used in this way. The person praying settles down quietly to saying calmly and repeatedly: 'Lord Jesus Christ, Son Of God, have mercy on me, a sinner.' Of course, the person praying does mean the words, but while the outer mind is occupied in reciting them, the 'deeper' mind or soul is left free to regard God, to believe in him, love him and be open to him. This might sound too mystical, but, in a slightly different way, since it also employs the imagination, it is only what pious people do when they recite the rosary.

4. The last way of using familiar prayers is to allow them to express our own spontaneous responses to God during the day or night. Novelists have attempted to represent the 'interior monologue' of human consciousness, though it seldom makes interesting reading. But if a human being is in the presence of God, there is an interior dialogue. Sometimes a verse of the Psalms, say, expresses exactly what one wants to say – as thanks, or petition, or praise, or contrition.

What remains true is that nothing whatsoever can prevent prayer. A mother constantly busy with children can still pray. Someone going through painful surgery can pray. If you are stuck on a coach journey with a video playing, you can pray. There are bound to be distractions, even in a quiet cloister. That is why eventually I settled on the title *Prayers for This Life*. This life is the one in which we learn to pray.

The mind still needs a supply of godly knowledge. To know prayers by heart helps, as does reading prayers that the best and holiest minds have contrived. Those are what I have looked for, and I hope others will find them useful.

16 OCTOBER 2004

A Private Diary

The medieval stone tower of Southwark Cathedral is hemmed in by elevated Victorian railway tracks and the dark arches of Borough market. Inside the church, it is peaceful, and to the right of the high altar stands an extraordinary Jacobean tomb. It was fashioned by the same sculptor who made Shakespeare's monument at Stratford, and in Southwark one sees a man in a dark cloak lying beneath a canopy with gilded pillars. An exuberant coat of arms surmounted by a golden mitre tops the whole thing.

The effigy is of Lancelot Andrewes (1555–1626), Bishop of Winchester. In his hands he holds a small book. People say the book is his celebrated *Private Prayers*. I bet it's not (since the prayers only became known publicly later), but perhaps it should be. Andrewes' great achievement was to head the committee that translated the first section of the 1611 Bible (Genesis to the Second Book of Kings). His own best-known words come in T. S. Eliot's 'Journey of the Magi'.

Andrewes had written of the Magi in one of his sermons on the Nativity: 'A cold coming they had of it at this time of the year, just the worst time of the year to take a journey, and specially a long journey in.' And those are practically the words Eliot put down in his poem. I like the 'in' at the end, as one says it in speech. Andrewes could write like that, in the pattern of language suitable for oral delivery. One of the audience was the king, and he would not have been disappointed.

But if that little stone book in the hands of the carved effigy is not the *Private Prayers*, we do have the real thing – a notebook bound in white vellum, five inches by two-and-a-half. It is in the Bodleian Library. In it, Bishop Andrewes wrote out detailed headings for his prayers, through the days of the week at regular times. The collection is written in Greek, a tongue that Andrewes loved as the language of the New Testament.

Andrewes gave the little book to William Laud, who became Archbishop of Canterbury. Laud had his head chopped off in 1645, but two years later the contents of the manuscript were published under the title *Private Devotions*. They were a bestseller among sympathizers with the learned, sacramental churchmanship of the so-called Caroline Divines. A new taste for just this sort of Anglican devotion grew in the first half of the nineteenth century, as part of the Oxford Movement. John Henry Newman, the vicar of the university church of St Mary's, where Laud had erected a pretty statue of the Virgin Mary under a canopy supported by stone, twisty barley-sugar columns, made a new translation of Andrewes' prayers. By then they were generally known under the Latin title of the *Preces Privatae.*

Now a selection has been made and translated afresh by the Rev. David Scott, *Andrewes: The Private Prayers,* (SPCK). Mr Scott is the editor of a series of books under the title 'The Golden Age of Spiritual Writing'. That is a reference to the seventeenth century, which was certainly a fine age for English prose. The important question is: can these prayers be used for my own prayer life? The answer is yes and no. No, because prayer is only each person's individual activity and openness to God. But yes, in that Andrewes' prayer headings suggest ideas that can be made my own prayer.

Andrewes is methodical. One of his schemes for a prayer of thanksgiving begins:

> O Lord, my Lord
> for that I am
> that I am alive
> that I am rational . . .

and it proceeds with 47 other headings before it bursts into praise and thanksgiving. He is also very biblical (while not spurning the traditions of the Orthodox or of the Latin Middle Ages). In one of his exercises on confession, he boils the prophet Habbakuk down to:

> I have heard the report of you and am afraid.
> I have considered your works and stand in awe.
> In your anger, remember mercy.

15 MAY 2004

What Anyone Can Do

I've been reading a remarkable book, which demonstrates that prayer is common to all humanity and more important than anything else. The book is by Ruth Burrows, for many years a Carmelite nun in rural Norfolk, and its title is *Essence of Prayer*. What struck me was her insistence that prayer is 'essentially what God does'. So this is emphatically not a 'how to' manual of prayer. Indeed, concentrating on a method can be a distraction, a displacement activity substituted for prayer.

What is prayer, then? St Teresa, the great reformer of the Carmelites, said it 'is nothing but friendly and frequent solitary converse with Him, who, we know, loves us'. As Ruth Burrows comments, 'God is not "out there" but most intimately present to me, in the blood pulse of my life. Our happiness is His happiness. He is engrossed with everything that concerns us, every detail of our lives, every cell of our bodies.'

In the face of God's penetrating love, there is no point complaining that 'I can't pray', or 'My prayer is hopeless' or 'I have never had anyone to teach me how to pray, and therefore I don't pray'. All that's needed is to 'allow ourselves to be loved, to be there for Love to love us'. But since this simple statement of God's love for each of us is too overwhelming for us to master, 'Most of the time we must accept it "in faith", as we say'.

A striking point in *Essence of Prayer* is that prayer is not discernible directly to our observation, even when we try to turn attention to the workings of our minds. One consequence is that we have no grounds for saying our attempts at prayer are 'getting nowhere' and none for thinking we are ascending some kind of ladder of improvement. God works unseen in us. 'It happens in darkness, hidden from the faculties,' says St John of the Cross. Only by our fruits can the working of the Holy Spirit be detected, and his effect on lives is to produce selflessness. (I can't say that I have noticed this in my own life.)

The conclusion must be, then, to 'Let God love you' in the formula of another amiable and intelligent woman, St Elisabeth of the Trinity, a Carmelite in Dijon who lived from 1880 to 1906.

I'm sorry to introduce just the names of these saints, but they knew what they were talking about.

To pray, then, and to let God love you, it is necessary to set aside time every day to be alone with God. It need not be a long time, but it is essential to keep it up, day after day, even when the time does not appear to have produced anything much but distractions and lack of feeling. To persevere in making yourself available to God is an exercise of faith, and in this life we can only know God by faith. It is not a matter of looking out of the window and wondering what's for lunch. To pray we can begin with a prayer, the Lord's Prayer, perhaps, or by reading a psalm. It is impossible to prescribe, for the spirit is radically free to follow the path that God is offering it.

But we cannot expect to have a meeting that is open to a loving God unless there has been some previous remote preparation. For a Christian, that means getting to know Jesus by reading the Gospels. It means reading other sound books to provide fodder for our minds. And it entails worshipping God with other people in the Christ-centred services of the Church.

This is not an exercise in ego-building, so the most illogical thing to do would be to expect agreeable 'experiences', even if they are 'religious' experiences. After all, what do we really want? If it is to respond to God's loving presence, then that is something anyone is free to do.

14 OCTOBER 2006

God's Rescue Plan

This week I found myself looking at an icon of Jesus in the Garden of Gethsemane. Christ, the Christian's exemplar, is praying for what confronts him that very day on which he lives, a man. He asks, if it is possible, not to have to go through the terrible experience of the Cross, but he adds, 'Not my will but thine be done.'

Now Jesus is God and he is man, but he is not God mixed up confusedly with a man. As God he loves and wants with the will of God; as a man he has a human will. In the seventh century, theologians tied themselves up in fearful knots trying to formulate this theologically, but it comes over with strong clarity in the drama of the Gospel narrative. In any case, it is not that God the Father wants a bad end for Jesus. He does not take pleasure in doing something bad to his only Son. God's will is free, but his choice is not between good and evil but between different courses of good.

We call 'providence' the choices that God makes, which bring good results from ill circumstances. Jesus, in conforming his own decisions as a man to those of God, holds fast to the rescue that God plucks from the wickedness attempted at the Crucifixion: the murder of God. The rescue plan is not just for Jesus, who rises as a man from the dead, but for all those with whom he is showing solidarity in choosing to undergo the death they have earned – in other words with every man and woman.

After his death, Jesus, as depicted by ancient Christian artists, plucks Adam and Eve by the wrists and pulls them from the graves they had dug for themselves. With that firm grasp they are uprooted from the dead earth and grafted as branches on to him, the vine. He is the new stock, the new Adam, from which all humanity draws life. All this is the happy consequence of Jesus's sorrowful prayer in Gethsemane. It also made it possible for us, as instructed, to pray the words 'Thy will be done' and to know that God's beneficent will for us is not thwarted. That prayer brings us within the rescue plan in this life.

God draws prayer out from us like a magnet. Christians are commanded to do something impossible for us: to love God with the whole heart. 'The act of prayer clarifies and purges our heart,' St Augustine writes, 'and makes it more capable of receiving the divine gifts that are poured out for us in the spirit.'

We possess an unquenchable thirst for the love of God. And yet when we let our buckets down on a string to fetch out the water to meet our thirst, all we get is a cupful at a time, it seems, if we are lucky. The Samaritan woman at Jacob's well had the same problem, and she heard the answer: 'The water that I will give will become in them a spring of water gushing up to eternal life.' In prayer we, like the Samaritan woman, engage Jesus in conversation, not quite understanding what he tells us.

18 JUNE 2005

Bowl of Cherries

Just as you are allowed to sit down without being able to define a chair, so, I'd have thought, you should be able to worship without being able to define religion. Even so, the theologian Keith Ward, in his new book *The Case for Religion* (Oneworld), does provide a definition of religion: 'A set of practices for establishing relationship to a supernatural or transcendent reality, for the sake of obtaining human good or avoiding harm.'

In academic circles it is better manners to say 'transcendent reality' than 'God', but there is another question that struck me about Professor Ward's definition. Is religion really practised 'for the sake of obtaining human good or avoiding harm'? Obviously it can be. As the juggernaut thunders down upon the pram in its path, a prayer or other quick impetrative act is a perfectly valid exercise of religion.

Chesterton, when climbing out of a period of pessimistic nihilism in his youth, found that his first religious acts were of gratitude, with no petitions attached. 'I had wandered', he recalled, 'to a position not very far from the phrase of my Puritan grandfather, when he said that he would thank God for his creation if he were a lost soul. I hung on to the remains of religion by one thin thread of thanks. I thanked whatever gods might be, not like Swinburne, because no life lived for ever, but because any life lived at all; not, like Henley, for my unconquerable soul (for I have never been so optimistic about my own soul as all that), but for my own soul and my own body, even if they could be conquered.'

There was no *quid pro quo*, no worship conditional on the reception of favours. I am not saying that it is wrong to seek to obtain good. Indeed, it is precisely because some of the best goods are gratuitous that we would do well to ask for them. The ability to play the piano can be obtained through constant practice, so they say, but the accomplishment of faith or hope comes no closer by making an effort. They are gifts that may be asked for. Please don't think I am saying that 'obtaining human good or avoiding harm' are not consequences of religion. It so happens that God by his nature overflows with good things. But I am not sure if one is allowed to know that, when playing

Professor Ward's game of 'establishing relationship to a supernatural or transcendent reality'. We might have to pretend that
we didn't know God is good.

Since he is, we can behave in a more confident way, just as we
can sit down more carefreely if we know that all four legs of the
chair are firmly attached. This optimistic attitude is reflected in
another book, which has whizzed into the *Church Times* Top 10.
It is *The Saints' Guide to Happiness* by Robert Ellsberg (Darton,
Longman and Todd). On the cover, the publishers have put a
picture of a bowl of cherries, which has sometimes been
described as 'what life is not'. But Mr Ellsberg is of a different
mind from the cynics. 'What', he asks, 'if happiness is not sub-
jective, a question of how we feel, or a matter of chance, something that simply happens? What if it is more like an objective
condition, something analogous to bodily health?' Aristotle, he
points out, took the latter view, and his word for happiness,
'*eudaimonia*', was a certain fullness of life, like the flourishing of
a healthy plant.

The quest of ancient philosophers was not to know whether
chairs or religion exist, but how human beings can be happy.
Perhaps after a while it becomes clear that the happiness for
which we yearn is not attainable here, now and by our own
efforts. Hence the need for 'establishing relationship to a supernatural or transcendent reality'. It looks as if what we ought to do
is, in any case, the very thing that is for our own good.

22 MAY 2004

A Lost Pet

I have before me a book called *I Love My Pet* by the Rev. Jude
Winkler (St Joseph Picture Books). It comes from America, with
36 colour pages. Near the beginning is a very rum picture
indeed. It shows Adam naming the animals – a doggy and a
smiling elephant and a giraffe and a frowning lion. The peculiar
thing is that Adam is wearing an animal skin. If you remember,
the naming of the animals came before the Fall, which was when
Adam began to wear clothes, and they were of fig leaves. An

animal would find it unsettling to be named by a man wearing an animal skin. I guess the image is influenced by a popular notion of 'cavemen'.

Then we get Noah's Ark. The two lions pictured going in are both male. That might just be ignorance on the part of the artist. Then there are scenes of the birth of Jesus (ox and 'donkey'), the Good Shepherd, Francis of Assisi, and after that we get on to pets. The general message is that we have a duty of care and must remember to clean out the mouse's cage. Trouble really comes on p. 28, with a prayer for a lost pet. 'Dear God,' it goes, 'I'm worried about my pet who is lost. I don't think that he/she will be able to take care of himself/herself, and I miss him/her terribly. You told us that You keep track of every sparrow in the sky and every lily in the field. So I know that You will also take care of X. Please send one of your Angels from heaven to guide X back to me. Thank You, Lord, because I know that You will hear and answer my prayer. Amen.'

Now, while it is quite likely that God will send one of his powerful angels to bring Fluff back, the parent must bear in mind that Fluff might already have been flattened by a lorry. In that case the exercise will end in the child thinking that God does not answer prayers. It could be the making of a little Richard Dawkins. Turn the page and the worst is fulfilled: 'Prayer for when a pet has died.' In a matter that means so much it would be more sensible to suggest a prayer that allows Providence to arrange things less specifically.

The common experience of Christians confirms that God does answer prayers. But no well disposed person would, for example, get a child to go through an exercise asking God miraculously to produce an ice-cream. This book is no worse than many others. That is the problem. And children are in no position to pick and choose.

24 MAY 2003

Online

All cultures practise prayer in a different manner, just as they have their own recipes, but in most it is a matter of course. The exception is the western urban culture, where most people can't be bothered to pray most of the time, and many do not know how to go about it even when they want to. The natural knack has been lost, as it has in dancing and singing, too – and eating is not what it was, either.

Preachers sometimes tell their auditors what busy lives they lead. But is that true? The average time spent watching television is more than 20 hours a week. Yet people find it hard to make room for ten minutes' prayer a day. What may be lacking is not time itself, but undistracted quietness. A recent experiment on the Internet (which itself has a tendency to obsess and distract users) has proved unexpectedly successful in countering this difficulty. The site is www.sacredspace.ie. I found it by typing sacredspace (one word) into the Google search engine.

It is designed to provide for ten minutes' prayer a day. Part of its attraction is that the user comes to it already prepared. 'A person at a computer has a sense of privacy and intimacy,' says Father Peter Scally, one of the team behind the site. 'Comfortable, upright and attentive, subconsciously filtering out distractions, he concentrates on the screen.' It is the kind of attitude of attentiveness enjoined by classical manuals on prayer.

The great thing is that people in an office or with a computer screen at home can concentrate on it for a few minutes without having to find refuge in an empty room. After all, plenty of other Internet activities take ten minutes. Click on the first page, and it leads you through six stages: 1. The presence of God; 2. Freedom; 3. Consciousness; 4. The Word; 5. Conversion; and 6. Conclusion. It is not at all as technical as that might sound.

On the first page, the user brings to mind that God is present, then clicks for the next page, Freedom. This unexpected stage entails asking God for help to turn one's desires to fuller love and life. Next comes a page for Consciousness – what Christians traditionally call examination of conscience, though here it is not linked merely to consciousness of sin.

The central exercise is on the page with the Word: a short

passage from the Gospel. After pondering it, there is an opportunity on the Conversation page to talk to Jesus Christ – not anything so twee or artificial as typing on the screen, but speaking silently in one's own mind. The concluding page takes you to an Amen, and that's it for the day. There is also help if the user gets stuck, with a blank mind.

The site follows the conventions of spirituality worked out by Ignatius Loyola (1491-1556). Many users, though, come from very different Christian traditions. Fr Scally is astonished by its popularity. My visit to the site, started in 1999, was its 5,391,524th. [When I revisited it in 2007 the total was more than 22 million.]

18 JANUARY 2003

Lady Godiva's Chaplet

When David Beckham stepped out to show off his plasterless foot after breaking a metatarsal, he was wearing a form of necklace that, on inspection, turned out to be a rosary. Though a taxi-driver often hangs a rosary on the rear-view mirror, it is an unusual form of ornament for a footballer. However, in about 1075, the famed Lady Godiva, who by repute could upstage even Beckham, left in her will, to a statue of the Virgin Mary in a certain monastery, 'the circlet of precious stones which she had threaded on a cord in order that by fingering them one after another she might count her prayers exactly'.

Indeed the antiquity of the custom is attested by the English word bead having originally meant a prayer, not a little round thing. In 885, Alfred the Great used the word in a book. Over the years, since people counted, or told, prayers on a rosary, bead became transferred from the prayer to the solid object. Like stairs or virginals, a set of beads was called a pair, as some still call them.

Counting prayers on beads or a knotted cord is common to several religions. Muslims, encouraged by the traditions of the Sufis, have a devotion to the 99 Names of God, which they count on a string of 99, or 33, beads. It is these that are often taken, by those content to be ignorant of Islam, for 'worry beads'. Marco Polo found the King of Malabar counting his prayers on beads, and St Francis Xavier in the sixteenth century was intrigued to discover them in use among the Buddhists of Japan. Monks and bishops of the Orthodox Churches carry beads too, to count prayers calling on Jesus for mercy.

What, though, was Lady Godiva counting on hers? Not Hail Marys, as the Catholics do today, for that prayer in its current form had not been invented in her time. No doubt she counted Our Fathers, or Paternosters. All over Europe in the Middle Ages sets of beads were called paternosters. Paternoster Row, next to St Paul's in London, was occupied by tradesmen who made them.

By the fifteenth century, these beads were known as rosaries, a word that merely meant a rose garden, literally or figuratively. By then, the devotion was fully developed; its aim was to allow contemplation of the Christian mysteries in turn – from the beginning of the earthly life of Jesus to the final bliss of heaven – accompanied by the recitation for each mystery of one Our Father and a 'decade' of Hail Marys.

Like Lady Godiva, a citizen of Morebath in Devon left her beads of coral and silver to the statue of Mary in the parish church (as Eamon Duffy notes in his recent book on the town). They were bought for 4s 10d by another woman parishioner so that the money could be spent on Mass vestments. The year was 1538, when beads were under attack from the authorities. But, in that year, no well-dressed woman would yet be without a pair of beads hanging at her belt. Devotion and fashion were inter-twined.

11 MAY 2002

Muddled Psalms

My paperback edition of the Psalms had fallen apart and I went to buy a new copy. It proved no easy task. The reason it had fallen apart is that I had been reading through it at a psalm a day – which gets you through the whole lot twice a year – and after a few years the glue had given way. Use of the Psalms in daily prayer is something that unites Christians, from Gaelic-speaking Calvinists on Skye to the Benedictines of Solesmes, and it also unites Christians with Jews, whose book, after all, it is. And, since psalms are recited in congregational worship, you get used to the translation adopted. This is where my trouble started.

I looked in the bookshop for the version we use in church. It happens to be one made, in 1962, by an organization called the Grail, intended to be amenable to recitation aloud or to singing. It is in wide use. But the version in the shop was the 'inclusive language' revision. I do not mean here to go into criticisms of inclusive language (which means that a translation gets round the stumbling block of using the male pronoun to signify both men and women).

But an example of the difference it makes is visible in the very first Psalm, which in 1962 ran: 'Happy indeed is the man who follows not the counsel of the wicked . . . He is like a tree that is planted beside the flowing water.' In the inclusive version, it is not one man but 'those', and 'they shall be like a tree'. Not 'trees', but 'a tree'.

It is a muddle. But muddle or not, it is not the version that is recited on Sunday mornings at my church. On enquiring, I found that the older version is out of print. Well, if I could not buy the version used at church, which version should I buy? The choice is bewildering. There is the Revised Version, the Revised Standard Version, the New Revised Standard Version Catholic Edition, the Jerusalem Bible, the International Version Anglicized Edition. That is before you go into the realms of the Good News Bible and beyond, where Saul is described as 'going to the bathroom'.

I bought the Authorized Version, otherwise known as the King James Bible. The shop assistant said: 'It's very inaccurate, you know.' But my criterion was not accuracy; it was to find a version that other people would be familiar with, one that is part of a common culture. I realize that most occasional church-goers are more familiar with the version of the Psalms found in the Book of Common Prayer, which is different from that in the Authorized Version. No matter; home Bible-readers know the Authorized Version.

At the same time, I bought a second-hand copy of the authorized Daily Prayer Book of the 'United Hebrew Congregations of the British Commonwealth'. It has Hebrew on the right, English on the left, based on a translation made by the Rev. S. Singer in 1890. I shall see whether unfamiliarity rather than congruity with habit gives these versions of the Psalms more impact for me or not.

21 SEPTEMBER 2002

5

Rites of Passage

In a Watery Grave

Andrew Marvell made a poetical piece of special pleading when he wrote: 'The grave's a fine and private place/But none, I think, do there embrace.' For the grave is nothing but a threshold, and over the threshold a man carries his wife with her body embraced in both arms. And when Mary embraces her cousin Elizabeth, the embryo John jumps in her womb, eager to leap from the grave of his nine-month watery burial.

Easter is all to do with the grave. In the year 391 St Ambrose explained it very clearly in a series of instructions to newly baptized Christians in the week after Easter. Baptism was death, he said, a watery grave, but death wasn't so bad. Men were created to live for ever, but they sinned and were cast out of paradise and became subject to death. What then? 'The Lord, who wished his gifts to last for ever, first passed sentence on man: "You are dust and to dust you shall return", and so he made man subject to death. The sentence was divine and could not be remitted by human kind.' Then came the remedy. 'It was that man should die and rise again. Why? So that what had formerly served as a sentence should now serve as a gift. And what is this but death? "How can this be?" you ask. Because death, when it comes, puts an end to sin.'

So that God's gift might continue for ever, 'man died but Christ invented the resurrection', says Ambrose. 'Death is the end of sin and the resurrection is the reformation of our nature.'

Yes, that's all very well, you might think, but isn't Easter to do with daffodils, lambs, chicks and new life? It is death killed, not burial alive. Perhaps, but nowhere speaks more about the resurrection of the body than the dour words of the burial service of the Book of Common Prayer: 'Earth to earth, ashes to ashes, dust to dust; in sure and certain hope of the Resurrection to eternal life.' Then Jesus Christ 'shall change our vile body, that it may be like unto his glorious body'.

If you did not expect bodily resurrection to eternal life, you were unwise to seek baptism in the first place, for baptism is no less than burial with Christ, being drowned in the baptismal waters and then fished out to a new life. *Boudu sauvé des eaux,* as the French film has it. 'When you are immersed,' Ambrose says, 'you receive the likeness of death and burial, you receive the sacrament of the cross; because Christ hung on the cross and his body was fastened to it by nails. Just so, you are crucified with him, you are fastened to Christ, you are fastened by the nails of our Lord Jesus Christ lest the devil pull you away.'

This sounds alarming. But the Christians of the ancient world regarded baptism as an awe-inspiring rite of initiation, whereas we regard it as a prelude to a tea party with sponge cake and frilly dresses. There were rival rites of initiation. The worshippers of Mithras had the taurobolium during which the initiate crouches in a pit covered with perforated boards over which a bull is slaughtered, so that its blood rains gushing on to the votary below. Baptism was never like that: 'You came into the baptistery, you saw the water,' St Ambrose said to the newly baptized. 'And if anyone should perhaps be thinking: "Is that all?", I say, indeed it is all.'

It is just water, as the Jordan was just water when Naaman the Syrian said, 'Is that all?' before he was cleansed by it of his leprosy. Just water from which Jonah was rescued. Just water that Jesus walked on and Peter sank into. It was just water that Jesus turned into wine. Just water that flowed from Jesus's pierced side on the Cross. The Red Sea was just water when the Israelites passed through it to a new life.

The door of the water's grave opens to a new world where old friends embrace again. Five fathoms down your father lies, but there is 'nothing of him that doth fade, but doth suffer a sea-change into something rich and strange'.

26 MARCH 2005

Brisbane's Fonts

Every convent girl knew that to baptize a baby (or anyone else who requires it) all she needed to do is pour water on its head while saying: 'I baptize you in the name of the Father and of the Son and of the Holy Spirit.' The exciting prospect was to win some dying child for heaven, or a Man Friday on a desert island for the Christian Church.

But now some priests in South Brisbane have been caught baptizing babies in the name of the 'Creator, Liberator and Sustainer'. The Archbishop of Brisbane has told them to stop. Diocesan authorities are worried that those baptisms are invalid. Fr Peter Kennedy of St Mary's, South Brisbane, disagrees and blames 'right-wingers' for denouncing him.

Baptism is a sacrament in common between the Catholic Church and the Anglican Church. The Prayer Book gives a form of baptism for babies, in conformity with the 27th of the 39 Articles, which sees 'the baptism of young children' as 'agreeable with the institution of Christ'.

The 1662 Prayer Book advises the priest to ascertain that 'the Child may well endure it' before he dips it in the water 'discreetly and warily'; but if it is weak 'it shall suffice to pour Water upon it', saying the given words.

The Prayer Book formula for baptism is taken from the Gospel according to St Matthew, where Jesus says: 'Go ye therefore, and teach all nations, baptizing them in the name of the Father and of the Son and of the Holy Ghost.' (Updated translations put 'Spirit' for 'Ghost' lest people think of scary ghosts.) Every few centuries someone dreams up a new heresy about baptism. In 1609, John Smith baptized himself, explaining why in *The Character of the Beast* (1610). He then changed his mind.

The Catholic Church ruled firmly during the Council of Trent in the mid-sixteenth century: 'If anyone says that baptism is optional, that is, not necessary for salvation, let him be anathema.' (The unbaptized were left to get into heaven by some sort of baptism of desire.) But in a sternly tolerant canon, Trent also shook anathema at anyone who denied that baptism given by heretics was valid. This was not new, since the Council of Florence in 1439 declared that even pagans could baptize validly, if they had the right intention. It didn't envisage self-baptism.

Matters of less moment have been made tests of orthodoxy. Under James I, the Church of England was torn between Puritans and traditionalists. Clerics' surplices were a shibboleth, and so was the use of the Sign of the Cross at baptism. The king called a conference in 1604 at Hampton Court, and a spokesman of the Puritans was John Knewstub (1544–1624). For 20 years he had protested about baptism as specified by the Prayer Book of 1559, with its rubric: 'The Priest shall make a Crosse upon the Childes forehead' (betokening 'that hereafter he shal not be ashamed to confesse the faith of Christ crucified'). When Knewstub went on at Hampton Court to denounce those who wore the surplice as no better than priests of Isis, he was rebuked by the king.

This use of the Sign of the Cross (repeated in the 1662 Prayer Book) was picked up in 1834 in No. 34 of the *Tracts for the Times*, which appealed to the Church Fathers, quoting Tertullian: 'If you demand a scripture rule for these and such like observances, we can give you none; all we say to you is that tradition directs, usage sanctions, faith obeys.' That tract was anonymous, but the author was John Henry Newman, vicar of St Mary's, Oxford, the university church. He once got into trouble for refusing to officiate in his church at the wedding of a woman who had not been baptized.

If you got Tertullian and John Knewstub and King James and John Henry Newman and even John Smith into a room and read the report of the Brisbane formula, I think they would be momentarily struck silent.

11 DECEMBER 2004

Vision of Magnus

In his best novel, *Magnus* (Canongate), the Orkney man George Mackay Brown has the martyr-hero connecting his own violent death with the whole history of salvation and sacrifice, through a rhapsody that takes in Cain and Abel, Abraham and Isaac and that strange figure Melchizedek.

Melchizedek is memorialized in a verse of the book of Genesis

(14.18): 'And Melchizedek king of Salem brought forth bread and wine: and he was the priest of the most high God.' The status that this obscure priest enjoyed in Judaeo-Christian culture is reflected in the Epistle to the Hebrews, where he is described as 'without father, without mother, without descent, having neither beginning of days, nor end of life; but made like unto the Son of God; abideth a priest continually'.

George Mackay Brown explicitly picks out his choice of vegetable offerings – bread and wine – as a parallel to the offerings of the Eucharist, of the Mass that St Magnus contemplates. The body and blood offered once for all by Jesus replace the bread and wine offered by Melchizedek, although in the Christian Eucharist the appearances remain.

With this in mind, it is fascinating to read some Bible study done by the Methodist scholar Margaret Barker, developed in *The Great High Priest: The Temple Roots of the Christian Liturgy* (Continuum). She likes to think that the Shewbread of the temple worship (an 'everlasting covenant', Lev. 24.8) is the remnant of an ancient non-animal temple sacrifice, of the kind offered by Melchizedek. Without accepting everything Dr Barker says (for she is celebrated as a maverick), it is enlightening to look at the Eucharist in relation to the Jewish Day of Atonement, rather than to the Passover as is usual.

Passover is celebrated in households, not by priests of the temple. But on the Day of Atonement, the High Priest enters the Holy of Holies. Again, there is some discussion of this, with reference to the priestly role of Jesus, in the Epistle to the Hebrews. But there is also evidence for the way in which the Eucharist shares characteristics of the Day of Atonement in early Christian writers such as Origen, and in the earliest liturgies, such as that of Addai and Mari (still used in Iraq), or of the fourth-century bishop Serapion.

Precisely how Jesus wanted to identify himself with Melchizedek is not a simple question. But the Jesuit theologian John McDade makes some vigorous criticisms of those scholars of the past 40 years who have played down Jesus's awareness of the salvific import of his own death.

Dr McDade quotes disapprovingly a woolly sentence from Edward Schillebeeckx's work from 1979, *Jesus: an Experiment in*

Christology: 'Jesus felt his death to be (in some way or other) part and parcel of the salvation-offered-by-God, as a historical consequence of his caring and loving service.' Schillebeeckx, Dr McDade laments, 'is unable to bring himself to say that Jesus saw his death as an offering for sins'.

But an awareness by Jesus of his inheritance of the priestly role of Melchizedek brings into focus a unified picture of the priestly work of the Day of Atonement, Jesus's own atoning death, and the history-piercing function of the atoning Eucharist.

5 NOVEMBER 2005

No Idolatry

The extraordinary Cambridge philosopher G. E. M. Anscombe died last week, and the obituaries hardly did her justice. (Obituaries never can.) Despite her standing as an explicator of Wittgenstein, with new insights of her own, she was unpopular with many philosophers for writing about religion, and she was unpopular with many of the professionally religious for taking doctrines seriously and treating them logically.

Before giving an example of the way she managed to *épater* both the philosophically and religiously bourgeois, it is worth noting her great achievement of clarifying the idea of intention. (Intention concerns what people mean to do when they perform actions.) Elizabeth Anscombe's analysis of intention incidentally throws stones at two sleeping dogs lying at the gates of public policy and private morality: utilitarianism and consequentialism. Utilitarianism was behind such policy documents as the Warnock report on human fertilization, which sowed a crop of horrors (clones and worse) now ripening. Consequentialism is behind the sort of do-it-yourself morality that smiles on euthanasia. The sleep of reason brings forth monsters.

Elizabeth Anscombe was no fundamentalist, but nor did she use philosophy to explain away the creed in which she believed. To an essay on the Eucharist, republished in the third volume of her collected philosophical papers (1981), she gave the title 'On Transubstantiation', even though the term substance was not one that her contemporaries or mentors used in their cosmology. The essay begins with the problem of explaining to a child the Real Presence of Christ in the Sacrament. 'When one says "transubstantiation", one is saying exactly what one teaches the child in teaching it that Christ's words, by the divine power given to the priest who uses them in his place, have changed the bread so that it isn't there any more (nor the stuff of which it is made), but instead there is the body of Christ. I knew a child', she continues, 'close upon three years old and only then beginning to talk, but taught as I have described, who was in the free space at the back of the church when the mother went to communion. "Is He in you?" the child asked when the mother came back. "Yes", she said, and to her amazement the child prostrated itself before her. I can testify to this, for I saw it happen. I once told the story to one of those theologians who unhappily (as it seems) strive to alter and water down our faith, and he deplored it.'

The story no doubt shocked, even if that paper was delivered to a Catholic audience. And, of course, Elizabeth Anscombe knew, as she went on to mention, that Christ is not present 'dimensively' (nor does transubstantiation imply that he is). She was only exemplifying what Dr Johnson noted: 'Sir, there is no idolatry in the Mass. They believe God to be there and they adore him.'

And now Elizabeth Anscombe has moved from the shadows and metaphors of philosophy into Reality, *ex umbris et imaginibus in veritatem.*

13 JANUARY 2001

Sister Death

What has it been like for the Pope, lying, dying, unable to speak but 'conscious, lucid and tranquil' according to the Vatican? What are these 'last rites' he received? The last sacrament that all Catholics wish to receive is Holy Communion. For those pilgrims or *viatores*, this sacrament has the name of '*viaticum*': 'way-bread' in appearance, the Body of Christ in substance.

In preparation for this last Communion, the faithful make their confession if they can. This Sacrament of Penance is normally made orally to a priest. If one cannot speak, as the Pope could not, other signs may be used. The minister makes everything as easy as possible for the penitent. The unconscious may receive conditional absolution from the priest.

The next sacrament of the three received on the deathbed is the Anointing of the Sick, formerly familiar as Extreme Unction. 'If any one of you is sick', wrote St James, 'he should send for the elders of the Church, and they must anoint him with oil in the name of the Lord and pray over him. The prayer of faith will save the sick man and the Lord will raise him up again; and if he has committed any sins, he will be forgiven' (Jas 5.14).

The sacrament has four effects. The first is the gift of the Holy Spirit, bringing 'strengthening, peace and courage' and forgiveness of sins, too. The second effect is union with the Passion of Christ. This is where television commentators go wrong. They say that Catholics prayed for the avoidance of suffering for the Pope. Perhaps some did, out of kindness. But the essential thing is that the suffering that dying always involves should be a participation in the saving work of Jesus. That is the point of being baptized into the death of Jesus at the beginning of a Christian life. The third effect is to 'contribute to the good of the People of God', as the Second Vatican Council said. The sick person, through this sacrament, contributes to the good of all mankind. We are with the Pope; he, or any dying person, is with us. No man is an island. The final effect of Extreme Unction is to fortify 'the end of our earthly life like a solid rampart for the final struggles before entering the Father's house'. The devil crouches like a lion by the bedside, eager to devour the poor soul on its way to God.

During the Sacrament, oil is put on the forehead and hands. People have been known to fear calling a priest for Extreme Unction lest it would upset the sick person. Those who have seen the effects of the sacrament realize this is the plumb wrong instinct, for the dying are left at peace and those who recover are strengthened for the fight.

Then comes Communion. If the patient cannot swallow the Blessed Sacrament under the form of bread, he may receive it under the form of wine. A drop suffices. Very wisely, the Pope decided not to go back to hospital. What would be the point? He was dying and knew it. No good would come from heroic measures to prolong life a few hours more.

Then comes death, 'Sister Bodily Death', as Francis of Assisi called her. The Pope has been a good man, and will not go to hell. But Catholics pray for the dead, as part of their belief in the Communion of Saints.

The prayer *In paradisum* is a commendation said by a priest over the recently dead body. In English, the words go: 'May the Angels lead you into paradise; may the martyrs greet you at your arrival and lead you into the holy city, Jerusalem.' It is rather moving.

2 APRIL 2005

6

Remarkable People

George Thomas of Soho

I've just come across the most extraordinary story, in a book that cost me 75p from a second-hand shop. It is called *George Thomas of Soho*, and the author was Dame Felicitas Corrigan, the friend of Siegfried Sassoon and biographer of Helen Waddell. It was published in 1970.

George Thomas's early life sounds like a parody of urban misfortune. His parents and their five children lived in three rooms on the second floor of 6 Berwick Street, Soho, above the market. The kitchen by day was the mother's bedroom by night. George (born in 1903), his mother, brother Dan and sister Ada developed muscular dystrophy. The father, an engaging but solitary man, took a job as a dustman – for the sake of the security. He worked nights and slept by day in the bed vacated by his two able-bodied sons.

So in that ten-foot by ten-foot kitchen, four crippled people sat, day after day, year after year, unable to get downstairs. George was lifted from bed to chair. One sink served the whole house. No sun shone in. The children's one trip out was as live specimens at a nearby medical school, at 3s 4d each. The family was truly poor, with tea and bread and one cooked meal a day if they were lucky. George, an angry young man, sometimes went to bed refusing supper, just to demonstrate he didn't care.

The crowded house was not all jolly cockney fun. One day George heard the Jewish woman living downstairs curse his brother for having accidentally knocked a jar of fish off her window-sill. 'May they all be paralyzed,' she shouted every few minutes. 'Because I'm only a bloody Jew, they knock my fish over.' The poor woman had the very washing stolen from her line by a visitor called Mary Ann. She would steal anything, even the door handles for scrap. One day she visited a blind woman in the tenement to sell her some tea, took her money, and stole back the tea. When Mary Ann visited the Thomases they made sure she sat by the wall, away from the spoons and forks. She died, still stealing, aged 84.

These details come from two books by George Thomas, *A Tenement in Soho* (1931) and a novel, *Neighbours* (1935). He wrote because of the encouragement of a woman called Erica Oxenham, who visited weekly, and got him to write letters. Later he took a correspondence course from the National Adult School Union. Before *A Tenement in Soho* was published, the tenement itself was being pulled down as unsafe. They had nowhere to go, sitting for weeks while the windows were taken out and the roof removed by demolition men. They got a council flat in Victoria, but were as poor and crippled as ever, and missed the market bustle.

Amid the grind and imprisonment, George Thomas's interior struggle continued. His faith in God, a faith taken as a datum in the family, withered in his bitterness. He felt utterly isolated. But from that he worked out an escape. 'In our solitary detachment, which no human effort can alter,' he wrote, 'we know that we can look on, and in looking on become aware of what we have to do and be. We have first to recognize the imperishable wonder of being, that we each have one window through which the infinite may be glimpsed.'

George Thomas was no academic. He was caught for a while in spiky misunderstandings about Christian doctrines. A touch of dark resentment in his writing is reminiscent of his embittered contemporary writer Denton Welch. But he grew to a position where he felt able to surrender to belief, willingly, because he was already in possession of life. He hated euthanasia; he preferred pain, immobility and dreariness because they were real. Most remarkably of all, he was befriended by a woman who did not feel sorry for him. They agreed to marry by letter, before they met. They met, and were married in 1943. Wheeled in a chair outside for the first time in 25 years, he remarked that, with his lolling head, he saw mostly grass.

George Thomas died in 1952, having found love.

26 FEBRUARY 2005

Canterbury Asian

In Istanbul, between the Cemberlitas tram stop and the Turkish baths, stands a smoke-blackened porphyry column, 100 feet high. It was put up by Constantine in AD 330, when it was a bit higher and topped by a statue of the emperor in the guise of the sun-god. In those days the column was surrounded by the forum and at its foot were preserved some of the imperial capital's most revered relics. Among them, according to St Theodore of Tarsus, were the 12 baskets used to gather the scraps after the feeding of the 5,000. They were woven from palm leaves, he reported.

Tomorrow is the feast of St Theodore (602–90). He ended up as Archbishop of Canterbury, a surprising appointment for an Asian from a far country. He got the job because it was turned down by an African, Hadrian. Those dark ages were quite enlightened racially. Canterbury was lucky to have Theodore, who made it the centre of the most accomplished school of biblical studies to flourish between the fall of Rome and the rise of the medieval universities. Theodore hoped to elucidate the Bible through the disciplines of philology and natural science. This was in the tradition of Antioch, on the river Orontes in Syria, just down the road from Tarsus. The rival school of Alexandria, in Egypt, specialized in allegorical interpretation, sometimes of the most surprising kind, to our eyes. Theodore was available to fill the see of Canterbury because his native land had been thrown into chaos by a double invasion, first in 613 by the Persians and then in 637 by the Muslim Arabs.

The Persians had taken the hallowed relics of the true Cross, which were recaptured in 627 by the Emperor Heraclius, an occasion marked each 14 September in the Christian calendar.

Heraclius turned out a bit of a disappointment, for he not only embraced the heresy of monothelitism, which wickedly denied that Christ had a human will, but went on to persecute anyone who refused to accept it. These included the best men around, such as Pope Martin and the admirable Maximus the Confessor, about whom Hans Urs von Balthasar wrote an enthusiastic book some years ago.

Theodore had gone to live in Rome, where several communities of eastern monks had taken refuge. There, in the 660s, a newly elected Archbishop of Canterbury called Wigheard had arrived to collect the pallium, the lambswool scarf given by the Pope as a symbol of authority. Poor Wigheard died of a fever and Pope Vitalian asked around for a substitute to send back. Hadrian the African, abbot of a monastery near Naples, having refused the post, suggested Theodore. Theodore, tactfully allowing his hair to grow into the form of tonsure more familiar to westerners, set off on 27 May 668, and arrived in England a year later. The Pope sent with him Hadrian and some relics of St Pancras. The church named after him later gave its name to a London railway terminal.

Theodore was already 67, a foreigner, and found a mess in England, where all but three sees were vacant. There was also a ticklish row between two men of strong character, both later recognized as saints, Chad and Wilfrid. Theodore had, at different times, to depose both from their bishoprics. Theodore's achievements in the 20 years or so left to him were organizational, doctrinal and liturgical. He summoned a synod, which embraced the orthodox Catholic teaching against the emperor's monothelitism. In 680, if Theodore had not been in his late seventies, he would have been summoned to the universal council at Constantinople.

As far as liturgy goes, he can lay claim to inventing the litany (with the *Kyrie Eleison* followed by invocation of the saints). The most extraordinary thing is that voluminous commentaries on the Bible deriving from Theodore remain unprinted, still languishing in manuscript after 1,300 years. I rather think Professor Michael Lapidge, the author of the standard work on Theodore, is at work getting more printed.

Theodore was buried at Canterbury Cathedral, though the exact spot has been lost. If anyone should be patron of racial harmony it is he.

18 SEPTEMBER 2004

A Saint to a Dinosaur

I am a dinosaur, C. S. Lewis told his audience in his inaugural lecture as a professor at Cambridge. 'If a live dinosaur dragged its slow length into the laboratory, would we not all look back as we fled? What a chance to know at last how it really moved and looked and smelled and what noises it made!' Lewis claimed to be one of the last living specimens of Old Western Man. He felt at home among the allegories and epics of the medieval and renaissance worlds. These were the sources for his *Narnia* books, with their fauns and monopods, dragons and centaurs, giants and sea serpents.

To Lewis, the most familiar texts were in Latin: Macrobius and Boethius, the *Historiarum Adversus Paganos* of Orosius and the *Utopia* of Thomas More. 'I read as a native texts that you must read as foreigners,' he said, meaning he shared the outlook of the authors. But it was his very literacy in Latin that led to a strange correspondence, from 1947 to 1954, with an Italian priest, Giovanni Calabria. I've just got hold of a copy of this curiosity (*The Latin Letters of C. S. Lewis*, translated and edited by Martin Moynihan, St Augustine's Press).

Calabria was 73 when the correspondence began, and had worked all his life to help abandoned children, the poor and the sick. (In 1999, he was declared a saint.) He wrote to Lewis after reading an Italian translation of *The Screwtape Letters*, in which Lewis had imagined a devilish correspondence between a junior and senior tempter. Calabria's first letter, from Verona, was dated 1 September, and Lewis's reply was immediate, dated 6 September.

Father Calabria hoped that in the 'ploughed-up field' (*aratus ager*) of postwar Europe, progress might be made to Church unity – *unitatem Corporis Christi, quod est Ecclesia*. Lewis replied that 'schism in the Body of Christ is both a source of grief and a matter for prayers, being a most serious stumbling block to those coming in, which also makes the faithful weaker in repelling the common foe'. Lewis explains he is no theologian, and prefers to leave aside the subtler questions about which the Roman Church and Protestants disagree, but in his books 'to expound those things which still, by God's grace, after so many sins and errors, are shared by us'. This had been the approach of Lewis's collection of wartime radio talks, *Mere Christianity*, a title he took from the eirenic Richard Baxter (1615–91), who had written, 'I am a Christian, a meer Christian, of no other Religion; and the Church that I am of is the Christian Church, and hath been visible where ever the Christian Religion and Church hath been visible'.

Lewis came to confide in his Italian correspondent. In a letter dated Boxing Day 1951 (or rather, *Die S Stephani* MCMLI) he writes: 'For a long time I believed that I believed in the forgiveness of sins. But suddenly (on St Mark's Day) this truth appeared in my mind in so clear a light that I perceived that never before (and that after so many confessions and absolutions) had I believed it with my whole heart.'

On 5 December 1954, Lewis wrote to tell Calabria about his appointment as professor of medieval and renaissance English literature at Cambridge. He had given his inaugural lecture the week before, under the title *De Descriptione Temporum* – though he spoke in English. 'The Christian faith,' he wrote now to the priest, 'counts for more among Cambridge men than among us; Communists are rarer and those plaguey philosophers whom we call Logical Positivists [*pestiferi philosophi quos logicales positivistos vocamus*] are not so powerful.'

'It will be a great delight to me if you write back to me again about yourself and your affairs,' Lewis concluded. But it was too late. Giovanni Calabria had died the day before.

3 DECEMBER 2005

China's Marco Polo

A Peking nobleman's son, who had become a monk and taught the people from a cave in the mountains, decided in the year 1275 to make a pilgrimage to Jerusalem. His name was Sauma, and he was a Christian of the Church of the East, the Syriac-speaking community with its centre in Mesopotamia, modern Iraq.

The Church of the East had a vigorous missionary life, and had established Christian churches in central Asia and China. But it had no communication with the Church in the West, either in Rome or Constantinople. Sauma travelled overland, joining the Silk Road at much the same time that Marco Polo was travelling in the other direction. With him, Sauma took a monk called Mark. To them, the wonders of the West, of which they left a record, were as strange as Cathay was to Marco Polo. When they reached Maragha, in what is now north-west Iran, they met Abaqa, the son of Hulagu, the Mongol invader. Hulagu is a name that Osama bin Laden threw into one of his tape-recorded diatribes, saying that Bush was a destroyer of the same stripe. It is not a name that rings a bell among most Britons, but Hulagu destroyed Baghdad in 1258. To an Iraqi he might sound like Hitler.

Hulagu was a grandson of Genghis Khan, and his brother was Kublai Khan (Coleridge's man), who became emperor of China while Hulagu set up in Persia. Their mother was a Christian, but like all successful conquering Mongols they had a fearsome reputation for slaughter. In any event, our pilgrims travelled on, failing to enter the Holy Land because it was under the control of the Muslim Mamluks. They tarried at Ctesiphon (20 miles from Baghdad), where the monk Mark was consecrated as a bishop by the patriarch of the Church of the East. The idea was that he could become Bishop of Cathay, but before they could return the patriarch died, and Mark was elected in his place, with the name Patriarch Yahballaha III. It was a strange choice, for Mark, now Yahballaha, had no Arabic and not much Syriac (a dialect of Aramaic). However, he knew the Mongols, who were then top dogs. (No one knew that Tamburlaine was just round the corner.) Yahballaha is said to have come close to converting the Tartars and their Turkic cousins to Christianity, which would certainly have shaken things up. Meanwhile, Sauma journeyed on, visiting Constantinople and Bordeaux, where he met Edward I of England. What an extraordinary bridge of worlds that was. Sauma seemed to think that Bordeaux was the capital of Angleterre – but Angleterre and Aquitaine must have seemed much the same after all he had seen.

The traveller was also received by Pope Nicholas IV, who invited him to take part in all the Holy Week ceremonies, and personally offered him Communion. This is of some importance, because there is a general idea that contemporary Christians of Mesopotamia or eastwards were incorrigible Nestorians, holding unorthodox ideas about the unity of Jesus Christ as God and man. In fact, most folk did not have the first idea that their faith differed in this from that of other Christians. The theologians were hampered by incompatible terminology and geographical isolation.

This needless doctrinal division is one theme of a fascinating new book by the Iraqi-born scholar Suha Rassam, *Christianity in Iraq* (Gracewing), a handy volume charting the glories and disasters of that land.

Even beyond the affliction of Iraq, the plight of the remaining Christians is distressing, and is now in a crucial phase. Christians have managed to survive there since the days of the Apostles. It would be more than sad if they were driven out partly because their story is less familiar to us than that of the pilgrim Sauma.

26 NOVEMBER 2005

Talking Eagle

One comment on the canonization of the sixteenth-century Indian Juan Diego by Pope John Paul last Wednesday came from a member of an evangelical sect in rural Mexico, as quoted by one of the international news agencies. 'He can't have been an Indian with a name like that,' the man said. 'An Indian would have had an Aztec or a Mayan name.' The comment exemplified the trivial level at which critics of the event have often been working: they focus on minor security scares, or object to the facial features of the images of Juan Diego. In fact, Juan Diego was the name by which the new saint was baptized, probably in 1524. His name in the Nahuatl language was Cuauhtlatoatzin, which means 'The Eagle that Talks'.

Although Protestant missionaries (often not from mainstream churches) are attracting a stream of converts in Mexico, the vast majority, perhaps 90 per cent of the population of 100 million, are Catholics. Most do not go to church every Sunday, but there was no doubting the popularity of the canonization. The enthusiasm was unmistakable in the crowds of Mexico City, which, with 24 million, accounts for a quarter of the nation's population. Police said that 4.5 million lined the road as the Pope drove to the Basilica of Guadalupe. Many were moved by his presence, on his fourth return to the country that was the first he visited in his 24-year pontificate. 'It's something beautiful and sad at the same time,' one young man in the crowd explained to a reporter. 'We are here to make our final farewell to this holy, courageous man.'

It was a remarkable performance for an 82-year-old with Parkinson's disease and bad arthritis, on a ten-day trip to Canada, Guatemala and Mexico. His message was simple: Juan Diego was a good man who had helped Mexico resist racial antagonism. 'He became the catalyst for the new Mexican identity, closely united to Our Lady of Guadalupe, whose mestizo face expresses a spiritual motherhood that embraces all Mexico.' The Mexicans still had the task of building a better country, though, 'with greater justice and solidarity'.

'Solidarity' is a word that John Paul has used all his reign. When he first visited Mexico, the people of Poland were opposing their communist rulers with a mass movement called Solidarity. 'Solidarity' is the heading of one section of a long document issued in 1999 after an international synod on the future of the Church in Latin America. There it was interpreted as the seeking of 'the good of others, especially of those in most need'. That contains the same nuance as the phrase 'preferential love for the poor', used by the synod instead of Marxist-inspired liberation theologians' idea of a revolutionary 'option for the poor' that sets them against the rest of society.

3 AUGUST 2002

Tragi-comic Life

Colonel Sibthorp, as he was universally known, became one of the tutelary figures of Michael Wharton's Peter Simple column in *The Daily Telegraph*. Charles de Laet Waldo Sibthorp was a diehard Tory who opposed the Reform Bill of 1832, succeeded in having Prince Albert's Civil List allowance reduced (principally because he was a foreigner), denounced the Great Exhibition of 1851 on the grounds that it encouraged foreign competition, anathematized railway trains for their encroachment on private property and ensured that the East Coast main line should not go through Lincoln, the constituency for which he sat until his death in 1855. But his brother Richard was far more eccentric.

Richard Sibthorp (1792–1879) was seldom sure for long that he was in the right Church. As an undergraduate he ran away from Oxford and sought out the Catholic bishop of the Midland District in Wolverhampton, from whose house he was fetched back after two days by an elder brother, with the assistance of the police. He settled to his studies again and was ordained a priest of the Church of England in 1819. In 1841, abandoning his congregation, he suddenly became a Catholic and was ordained a Catholic priest. Within 18 months, after an accident where a gig in which he was riding overturned and he hurt his head, he reverted to the Church of England, having to wait a few years before he was allowed to minister again. By now he was in an inner torment, missing what he had left, fearing to return, unsatisfied by what he embraced. 'God knows how I have felt the change from Rome to Anglicanism!' he was to write to J. R. Bloxam, once Newman's curate at Littlemore. 'I have scarcely known a day of mental or heart peace since I made it.'

More than 20 years later he once again took up the duties of a Catholic priest, by chance choosing the days of Cardinal Wiseman's rococo last illness. As Wiseman endured painful operations and arranged full-dress last rites at his bedside, Sibthorp celebrated his first Mass for 20 years in the next room. When Sibthorp's turn came to die, in his 87th year, it was also after receiving the last rites of the Catholic Church, but having stipulated that he should be buried with the words of the service from the Book of Common Prayer read over his grave.

Sibthorp met the great religious characters of his day and exemplified many of the oddities of the period. These appear in the new, extremely well researched, *Life of Richard Waldo Sibthorp* by Michael Trott (Sussex Academic Press), better than anything written about him before, and a treat for connoisseurs of eccentricity. We find Bishop Samuel Wilberforce, for example, alarmed at a curate intending to install a stone altar and a brass eagle lectern in his church: 'Let me remind you that the introduction of these was a prominent step in poor Sibthorp's unhappy career.'

But Dr Trott convincingly identifies Sibthorp's leading appetite as the pursuit of holiness. It was this that drew him to co-operate with Methodists in his earliest Church of England ministry. It attracted him to the idea of the Indian missions, it turned him into an energetic evangelical preacher of forceful influence. It inspired him, once he had bought a proprietary chapel at a fashionable watering place on the Isle of Wight, to establish full choral services and to transform its fittings – that eagle and worse. Sibthorp had his fears, too. He turned away again from the Catholic Church out of fear that it was the Antichrist of the book of Revelation. He was an intense but not a systematic theologian, being taken by surprise in mid-life by a straightforward explanation of baptismal regeneration. He could never reconcile himself to what he saw as Mariolatry, worship of the Virgin Mary.

Unworldly, despite commanding the resources to buy a chapel here or build a set of almshouses there, he never acquired the knack of joining with others in action and common belief. His story is at once deeply pitiful and richly comic.

15 APRIL 2006

A Barbastro Boy

A poster on the door of the great Basilica of El Pilar in Zaragoza advertises the declaration tomorrow week of the sainthood of Josemaria Escrivá, founder of Opus Dei. As a boy he lived in Barbastro, up the road, and spoke, I am told, with an Aragonese accent. I never thought I should live to see this event. I met him once, in Rome, and one does not expect people one has met to be canonized, partly because of the time the process takes. But the real reason I didn't expect this canonization was ideological. I don't mean that Josemaria Escriva – St Josemaria in a week's time – had an ideology that should have debarred him from the company of the saints. Quite the opposite: he was clearly a saintly man. It was the ideology of his opponents that I thought would delay his canonization.

If Blessed Josemaria (as he is for the next few days) had a reputation of any kind in Britain, it was as a very Catholic Catholic. And since Catholicism is often seen by a liberal culture as reactionary, so was Josemaria Escrivá, and the organization he founded. But tension among Catholics was of a quite different kind, for Opus Dei was not reactionary in Catholic terms, but revolutionary. As an association run largely by lay people for lay people, it seemed, to parts of the clericalized establishment, to challenge a rather patronizing attitude to the laity. That challenge was not made intentionally by Opus Dei, but it was resented. A 'church within a church' was how some characterized it.

The Roman Catholic Church itself came to see things differently. The Second Vatican Council in the early 1960s endorsed the message of Opus Dei that lay people should seek holiness in the world, through the pursuit of their secular tasks, by virtue of their vocation as baptized Christians. The Second Vatican Council was at the same time invoked by all sorts of trendy experimentalists – at least its 'Spirit' was invoked, since it was impossible to find in its conclusions any justification for many of the fringe practices embraced in the years that followed.

Anyway, *bien-pensant* theologians and committee-men did not fancy Opus Dei one bit, in the three decades following the council. I came across some breathtaking prejudice in the 1980s when I was a member. It was like anti-Semitism: you were presumed guilty for what you were, not what you did. To be fair, members of Opus Dei in Britain may have given a strange impression by exhibiting a predominantly Spanish culture. They hardly knew this, as it came naturally, and nor did I, since I had never visited Spain in those days. Not that I have found subsequently that Spanish culture is such a bad thing. In the meantime, Opus Dei has become 'inculturated' in Britain, as theologians would say. It always hated racism and is raising funds to back a social project in Africa to mark this canonization.

In the universal Church, other lay movements are growing too. The Pope is encouraging them. The time is propitious and in Rome on 6 October, 74 years and four days after he founded Opus Dei, Josemaria Escrivá will be declared a saint.

28 SEPTEMBER 2002

Debt to the Poor

A great stir followed a declaration by Cardinal Manning that a starving man was not stealing if he took the food he needed from his neighbour. The natural right to life and food, he said, prevailed even over the laws of property. It was 1887, and the laws of England were harsh enough against poachers and those who took things that belonged to others. Property was hedged about by fierce judges and policemen. Manning's remarks sounded like the subversive message of the Christian Socialists.

In fact Manning was only following traditional Catholic teachings. It is just that Catholic social teaching was very unfamiliar to the English in the 1880s. Nor was the ascetic, patrician-looking Cardinal Archbishop of Westminster undergoing a sudden conversion. 'The thought of our destitute millions,' he had written in the 1840s to the sister of F. D. Maurice, the founder of Christian Socialism, 'and of the hard hand which too often converts charity into chastisement on the poor is enough to make one's heart sicken.' While still Archdeacon of Chichester, in the Church of England, Henry Edward Manning had declared: 'It is a high sin in the sight of Heaven for a man to wring his wealth out of the thews and sinews of his fellows, and to think that when he has paid them their wages he has paid them all he owes.'

These same ideas are discernible in a new book from the Pontifical Council for Justice and Peace, which is part of the Roman Curia. It is called *Compendium of the Social Doctrine of the Church* (Burns & Oates), and in a snappy 426 pages it sets the main points in context. Echoing the Protestant Archdeacon of Chichester 160 years ago, the compendium makes it clear that the poor deserve more than charity: 'When we attend to the needs of those in want, we give them what is theirs, not ours. More than performing works of mercy, we are paying a debt of justice.' And those are not words that the Romish cardinals have just invented. They are quoted from St Gregory the Great, the man who sent Augustine of Canterbury to bring Christianity to our English forebears. They come in his *Pastoral Care*, a book later translated into English by King Alfred the Great and circulated by him to the bishops of his realm.

The bishops of the Second Vatican Council in the 1960s

agreed. 'What is already due in justice,' they pronounced in the decree *Apostolicam Actuositatem*, 'is not to be offered as a gift of charity.' Indeed the duty in justice to give food, drink, clothing and shelter to the poor is, in the Gospel according to St Matthew, the very criterion at the last judgement. 'I was hungry,' Jesus says to those cast into hell, 'and you fed me not.' Every schoolchild used to know from the *Penny Catechism* that two of the four 'sins that cry out to heaven for vengeance' are oppression of the poor and depriving the labourer of his wages. (The other two are wilful murder and the sin of Sodom, but never mind those for now.) It is no good the rich pretending that they don't know their duty in justice; they'll find out soon enough.

The *Compendium*'s principle of the 'universal destination of goods' (that they should meet the common good) is applicable to public policy as well as private plans. In an encyclical letter marking the hundredth anniversary of the great social encyclical of Leo XIII (*Rerum Novarum*, much influenced by Manning), Pope John Paul wrote: 'It is necessary to break down the barriers and monopolies which leave so many countries on the margins of development.'

He was writing about principle, not political details. It is for those who can influence it to examine the agricultural policy of the European Union, for example, and see whether it is a barrier to the development of poor people outside it.

And, talking about principles applicable to the EU, one of the axioms defined by the new compendium is 'subsidiarity'. It might not sound pretty, but it is a nice sharp instrument for deflating overblown centralized power.

11 JUNE 2005

Sharp amid Disaster

Chance and temperament made the life of Peter Anson something of a disaster. When I mentioned his name a few weeks ago in connection with missions to seafarers, I did not think he'd be in the news again so soon. But an introduction to his life called *Peter Anson: Monk, Writer and Artist* has just been written by Michael Yelton (Anglo-Catholic History Society). Anson (1889–

1975) wasn't in fact a monk – or not for very long. His father was an admiral, but he was never sent to public school, since his health was deemed too delicate. He was not to go to university either, instead building up an extraordinary knowledge of ritualistic worship.

He lodged with the (High Anglican) Cowley Fathers in Westminster while attempting to study at the Architectural Association. On a Sunday he might attend early Holy Communion, then the office of Prime, and, after breakfast, Terce. Then he would go out to sample Divine Liturgy at the Russian embassy chapel. After None with the Cowley Fathers, he would set out for Solemn Vespers and Benediction at the Roman Catholic cathedral at Westminster, before returning home for Compline. There was always the chance of a more recherché visit, perhaps to the Catholic Apostolic church in Gordon Square. To many it would seem an unhealthy obsession. For Anson it led in 1910 to an attempt to join the life of a monastic experiment in the Anglican Church, at the newly founded community at Caldey Island off Pembrokeshire. This was under the sway of that strange figure Aelred Carlyle.

Carlyle was impulsive and impractical, single-minded and happy to run up ever-growing debts. He persuaded Lord Halifax, among others, to back him, and he persuaded himself that the religious practices at Caldey – Mass in Latin, Benediction of the Blessed Sacrament and so on – were consonant with the laws of the Church of England. It could not last, and in 1913, led by Carlyle, the community (bar a handful) joined the Roman Catholic Church, Anson with them. But two things militated against Anson settling down as a monk. One was his lifelong 'neuraesthenia' – a term in his time for neurosis or anxiety – another was his love of the sea, sailors and the wandering life of a mariner.

As for Carlyle, Anson wrote a biography of him that showed his faults cruelly – his vanity, favouritism, unintegrated sexual preferences (even if not played out fully), his underlying refusal to face monetary reality. Anson always had a fundamentally subversive pen, which he also turned to comic account against Fr Ignatius, the nineteenth-century founder of the do-it-yourself monastery at Llanthony. Of course it was true that these pioneering monasteries were beset by chaos, human frailty, sometimes crime, and their founders were men of marked character, given to making the world revolve around themselves. In a saint, with the support of a church, these characteristics might have laid foundations on which others could build. With Fr Ignatius and Carlyle, they led to collapse.

In his fascination with the oddities of these men, Anson is also examining his own divided inclinations. For the rest of his life he drifted around Scotland and Europe, sometimes at sea, sometimes drawing, always writing, seldom persevering with any strictly scholarly research. One of his best books is *Fashions in Church Furnishings: 1840–1940*, which surveys the development of Catholic practices in the Church of England and Scottish Episcopal Church, as seen through the building of churches and their adaptation to different kinds of liturgy. Its early chapters rely heavily on that opinionated old periodical *The Ecclesiologist*, but without Anson's own wide understanding of worship none of it could have been put into a pattern. His meticulous drawings add much to the analysis.

Perhaps the most impressive thing Anson did was on separate occasions to nurse two men through terminal illnesses in his own home. As a monk he failed, and he was no model for a layman, but we must be grateful for his observant drawings and sharp pen.

19 November 2005

Martyr in Greeneland

Graham Greene saw the world through Left-wing spectacles and Evelyn Waugh through the lenses of the Right. But both agreed about the Mexican martyr Miguel Pro, the anniversary of whose death falls on Thursday.

Waugh visited Mexico in 1938 and described his experience in *Robbery Under Law*; Greene had travelled there separately in the same year and wrote about it in *The Lawless Roads*. His great novel *The Power and the Glory* is also set in a Mexico of merciless persecution. Waugh had recently published an award-winning biography of the Elizabethan martyr Edmund Campion, and in a preface to *Robbery Under Law* he noted that 'the martyrdom of Father Pro in Mexico re-enacted Campion's in faithful detail'. Like Campion, Pro (born in 1891) was a member of the missionary Society of Jesus and, because of anti-Catholic laws, he had had to train as a priest abroad. He returned to Mexico in 1926 just as President Plutarco Elias Calles was promoting a more violent state repression of Catholic life. Priests were arrested, tortured and executed just for baptizing children, saying Mass or giving the last rites to the dying. As Graham Greene wrote: 'We know how Pro was dressed when a year and a half later he came out into the prison yard to be shot, and he may well have worn the same disguise when he landed (the equivalent of Campion's doublet and hose): a dark lounge suit, soft collar and tie, a bright cardigan. Most priests wear their mufti with a kind of uneasiness, but Pro was a good actor.'

Reading about Miguel Pro is to find a culture very much of its period, when secular life was inspiring Christians to adopt modern methods. Pro and his friends were joky, keen, fit, disciplined, self-sacrificing, eager to help the poor, studious and un-cynical. To the English-speaking reader they have the air of boy scouts. But they were prepared to meet death in their good deeds. 'In the poor quarters,' Pro wrote, 'I seemed to have found myself in my element. I talked, even shouted, before that audience in shirt-sleeves. Hundreds came to our spiritual talks, braving the police. They were poor people, too!'

Dodging the police who sought his life, Pro gained a reputation for daring. He sometimes improvised disguises, as a workman or, once, as a young man with his fiancée. I had previously been doubtful about Miguel Pro, because he died in the year of a rebellion in Mexico led by the so-called Cristeros, with their watchword '*Viva Cristo Rey!*' – 'Long Live Christ the King!' The Cristeros are portrayed as violent obscurantists by the secularist Left and Right. As far as I can make out, though, it was quite proper to rebel against the vile Mexican regime. In any case, Pro did not join the Cristeros. For him, Christ was King in the kingdom that Christians pray for in the Lord's Prayer.

When his superiors told him to lie low, he protested: 'The people are in dire need of spiritual help. Every day I hear of people dying without the sacraments. Priests are no longer ready to court danger.' He promised to be careful. 'They got him, of course, at last,' Greene wrote. After a dynamite assassination attempt on General Alvaro Obregon (a retired president), Pro and his brother Humberto were arrested and interrogated. There was no question of a trial. After a bad night in a cold cell, Pro's head ached and he took an aspirin someone had given him. He and his brother tried to warm themselves up by practising some juggling. Not long afterwards, they were led out to the firing-squad. Pro was able to kneel for a minute in prayer, then, refusing a blindfold, he stretched his arms out in the shape of a cross and faced the firing-squad. 'May God have mercy on you,' he said. 'May God bless you. Lord, you know that I am innocent. With all my heart I forgive my enemies.' His last words were: '*Viva Cristo Rey.*'

In a propaganda exercise that went wrong, as Greene noted, he was 'photographed by the official photographer, praying for his enemies by the pitted wall, receiving the *coup de grâce*; the photographs were sent to the press – to show the firmness of the Government – but within a few weeks it became a penal offence to possess them'. Thousands crowded the streets at his funeral, defying the authorities.

Miguel Pro was beatified by Pope John Paul II in 1988. In Mexico City the site of his martyrdom is now marked with a little plaque, half hidden by some ropy electrical wiring, next to a shop in the Calle Loteria Nacional.

18 November 2006

7

Living Creatures

Food to Jump At

Locusts were the hot topic with which *The Daily Telegraph* letters columns were swarming this week. Did John the Baptist eat 'locusts and wild honey' as the Bible seems to say? Barry Fantoni, the cartoonist, insisted that the Baptist ate the pods of the locust tree. For this opinion he gains some support from the *Oxford English Dictionary*, which says: 'The Greek name *akris*, properly denoting the insect, is applied in the Levant to the carob-pod, from some resemblance in form; and from very early times it has been believed by many that the "locusts" eaten by John the Baptist were these pods.'

But by the same token, *akris* is the word used in the Septuagint version of the Old Testament to signify the hopping insect, and is not used elsewhere in the Bible to mean a pod. There was no disgust or religious scruple in eating locusts. Leviticus says: 'Even these of them ye may eat; the locust after his kind, and the bald locust after his kind, and the beetle after his kind, and the grasshopper after his kind.' That is the Authorized Version. Entomologists identify them as: locust, katydid, cricket and grasshopper. The criterion is that, as well as having four legs to walk, the creatures should have another pair for jumping as a grasshopper or locust has.

Much popular opposition to John's locusts is fuelled by the Internet. One argument is that *akris*, the word in the Gospel, should be *enkris*, meaning 'cake'. The learned Dr Peter Jones, of Friends of Classics, tells me there was in ancient Greek culture a cake called *enkris* boiled in olive oil and soaked in honey. Athenaeus in *The Deipnosophists*, that great hotchpotch of dinner-table lore, mentions it several times, once served as a sort of dessert together with roast thrushes. Such cakes were also sold by street vendors. They sound like a sticky Mediterranean pudding to be served with Turkish coffee. I haven't yet seen it suggested that John drank coffee too.

So *enkris* seems too much of a delicacy. In the Greek translation of Exodus (16.31), manna is described as being like '*enkris en meliti*', 'cake in honey'. But John went about in camel hair, not as a luxury fashion item but as a desert austerity. In any case, no manuscript of the Gospel according to Mark or Matthew has *enkris* as a variant reading. All say *akris*, 'locust'. It was meat, of a sort, and not a sweet. However, opposition to the locust also comes from recruiters of John to vegetarianism. Some Seventh Day Adventists, who favour vegetarianism, seek this. It is not clear why. John might indeed have abstained from flesh meat, though I cannot see that he would refuse the ritual Passover lamb. But you can hardly count a locust as flesh meat. It does not have to be slaughtered in a ritual way; its blood does not have to be drained.

To argue from statements about early Christians refraining from meat is beside the point. We know why that was. Meat readily available in Mediterranean countries at the time was likely to have been sacrificed to a pagan deity and so, as St Paul counsels, would be no-go even for those who had jettisoned the distinction between clean and unclean meat. 'The unnatural eating of flesh,' says a fragment of Papias (reputed to have known St John the Evangelist), 'is as polluting as the heathens' worship of devils with its sacrifices and impure feasts, through participation in which a man becomes a fellow eater with devils.'

Yet there was, clearly, an early ascetical practice of forgoing flesh meat, along with alcohol, as a penitential habit of life. 'The apostle Matthew partook of seeds and nuts, fruits and vegetables but not flesh,' wrote Clement of Alexandria, who died about the year 215. 'And John, who carried temperance to the extreme, ate locusts and wild honey.' To me, that indicates not that the locusts were vegetables but that locusts were a windfall desert food. Jews in Yemen are said still to eat them, fried. Only about 300 Jews survive in Yemen, so there should be plenty to go round.

4 SEPTEMBER 2004

Birds of Heaven

The centre of Newton Abbot in Devon has been recommended to birdwatchers who want to see large numbers of pied wagtails roosting. In Britain we are used to having birds about the place. Like mammals, they are creatures of which we take note.

Small and creeping things we eradicate indoors and disregard outdoors. Mammals we domesticate or hunt, either as vermin (rats, foxes) or as dangers (bears, boars). But birds we can manage to live with. If they eat our crops we shoot them; if we can eat them, and they're large enough, we also shoot them. Otherwise, they come and go as they please, cautiously and at a distance. Though people call pigeons 'winged rats', they do not loathe them quite in the same way. It helps that birds, like fish, belong to a different element. Not only can they escape by air, but there they encounter us less. They may even benefit from the gardens that men make.

Wild birds are a reminder from God that other creatures on earth have an independent way of life. They are an image of freedom and deliverance: 'Our soul is escaped as a bird out of the snare of the fowlers: the snare is broken, and we are escaped' (Psalm 124). Birds enjoy a generally positive treatment in the Bible. 'The sparrow', says the Psalmist, 'hath found an house, and the swallow a nest for herself, where she may lay her young, even thine altars, O Lord of hosts, my King, and my God.' They are shown as having a direct relationship with God, their creator. This providential care is taken up by Jesus in the words reported by Matthew (10.30): 'Are not two sparrows sold for a farthing? And one of them shall not fall on the ground without your Father. Fear ye not therefore, ye are of more value than many sparrows.'

'Behold the fowls of the air,' he tells his disciples, 'for they sow not, neither do they reap, nor gather into barns; yet your heavenly Father feedeth them. Are ye not much better than they?' When Jesus speaks of his own poverty – implicitly a reliance on providence – he says: 'The foxes have holes, and the birds of the air have nests; but the Son of man hath not where to lay his head.'

In the Authorized Version, the regular phrase is 'the birds of the air', and that alone gives them their own dominion. But in the Latin version made by St Jerome in the fourth century, they are called *volucres* or *volatilia caeli* – the birds of heaven. In the account that Genesis gives of the Creation: 'The Lord God formed every beast of the field, and every fowl of the air; and brought them unto Adam to see what he would call them: and whatsoever Adam called every living creature, that was the name thereof' (2.19). One of the lovely carvings on Chartres Cathedral shows God, depicted not as an old man with a long beard, but as a young man, bringing Adam the birds to be named.

Respect for wild birds was a teaching of our own English saint, Bede (673–735), who derived it partly from his master St Cuthbert. In his biography of Cuthbert, Bede tells the story of how he set off for a far village to preach. The boy who accompanied Cuthbert admitted he was wondering where they could stop in the empty Northumberland countryside to find something to eat. 'My son,' Cuthbert said, 'learn to have faith, and trust in God, who will never allow those who trust in him to perish with hunger.' Then looking up, they saw an eagle in the air. Cuthbert said: 'God could feed us even by means of that eagle.' As they were talking, they came near a river, and saw the eagle standing on its bank. 'Look, there is our good servant the eagle,' Cuthbert said. 'Run, and see what provision God has sent us, and come again and tell me.' The boy ran and brought back a good-sized fish, which the eagle had just caught. But the saint reproved him: 'What have you done, my son! Why have you not given part to God's servant? Cut the fish in two pieces, and give her one half, as her service deserves.'

I hope the wagtails of Newton Abbot are treated so well.

31 DECEMBER 2005

Bats, not Rats

Last year, when *Telegraph* readers responded to the question 'Are bats welcome in church?' the bats lost, but only by a margin of 3:2. Bats are a popular variety of God's creatures. If the question had been 'Are rats welcome in church?' the outcome would hardly have been so close.

Now bats are staining the font and rotting the altar rails at the Saxon church of St Hilda's, Ellerburn, near Pickering, Yorkshire. Pevsner is enthusiastic about the architecture. As the *Telegraph* reported on Tuesday, parishioners are upset because they are not allowed to stop the creatures coming into the nave and making a mess. Some parishioners think the bats spread food poisoning with their droppings. Bat excrement also contains urea, an organic compound that has the same effect on brass or textiles as ammonia. 'It is now impossible for us to clear up the mess,' says Rachel Grimble, 79, one of the voluntary cleaning ladies at St Hilda's.

Bats are protected under the Wildlife & Countryside Act, 1981. No one would put up with bats posing a health risk at home, but the problem is that English Nature is the statutory body designated to decide what can be done about bats in churches. English Nature seems to guard its privileges jealously. Its 76-page *Bat Mitigation Guidelines* are intended to mitigate not the effects of bats on people, but the effect that mending buildings has on bats. Even if a special licence is obtained from Defra, after complicated and sometimes expensive application provisions, 'the applicant must demonstrate there is no satisfactory alternative and that the action will not adversely affect the favourable conservation status of the bats'. It uses a similar tone to family legislation in which 'the interests of the child are paramount'.

St Hilda's is thought to shelter about 30 female breeding Natterer's bats, a rare species, among other bats also in the church. Rarity is a relative term. St Hilda's score or two Natterer's bats join each winter perhaps 5,000 hibernating in the nearby Ryedale Windy Pits caves. Ordinary bats at St Hilda's live to everyone's satisfaction in the roof space, but the Natterer's bats enter through a narrow gap at the side of the door, flying into the nave. 'The problem could be solved in minutes with a bit of rubber costing a few pence,' says John Grimble, the church's bat officer. Sealing the gap in winter would stop the bats returning to the same nesting site. 'But the strict laws, made by the British and EU officials to protect bats, forbid sealing any entrance point.'

Some people won't come to services at St Hilda's any more, because of the bats. Even closure is contemplated. 'Clearly, the law is unfair,' says Dr David Galliford, a retired bishop who lives in the combined benefice of All Saints, Thornton Dale, with Allerston, Ebberston, Ellerburn and Wilton. 'It gives bats far more rights than humans – and no one can accept this when it threatens to drive people out of a church and close it.'

When the Movement Against Bats in Churches was founded 12 years ago by Catherine Ward, a clergy wife, she received a flood of mail from 17 dioceses. 'Ours is a small Saxon church, with some of the finest wall paintings in England, which the bats are ruining,' said one letter. English Nature officials advise steps such as putting covers over church furnishings. But covers for pulpits, memorials, rails, fonts and pews are not easily arranged, and who wants to remove them before services when they are covered with droppings?

In any other country the law would be ignored as foolish, and bats banned from the interiors of churches.

1 MAY 2004

Chickens in Church

I wonder where the chickens are?, I thought as the cathedral service ended. I turned to go, and there they were all the time, eyeing me from their perch, in the sideways, unengaged way chickens have – fine creatures, a cock and a hen, big and white with red battlements. The pair live behind baroque wrought-iron bars with gilt curlicues, in a stone loft 12 feet up on the west wall of the south transept of the Cathedral of Santo Domingo de la Calzada in La Rioja, northern Spain. No one had told me it was the saint's feast day this week. Usually I avoid Spanish fiestas – one is not part of the local community and becomes a voyeur. In any case, though half the town is drunk, it is impossible to get served, and everything is closed.

As for the chickens, let's do the story briskly: a pilgrim to Santiago was framed by a wicked barmaid, who hid a silver cup in his pack. So he was hanged. His parents, passing his body on the gallows, heard him say he was still alive, thanks to the intercession of Santo Domingo. They went to the magistrate. He was tucking into a couple of roast fowls and said: 'He's no more alive than these chickens' – at which the cock and hen leapt up clucking and crowing. The youth was cut down and everybody lived happily ever after.

St Dominic of Calzada did not become a saint because of this wonder. He had been dead some years by then, having lived from 1019 to 1109. He had made the bridge (18 arches) over the River Oja (of Rioja) and a causeway (calzada) to ease the way for pilgrims to Santiago. During the fiesta, there was a strange procession of 24 *doncellas* (damsels) in veiled hats like wedding cakes, and the statue of the saint was carried aloft by 12 men, and to a drum and reedy pipes 13 boys in red and blue danced (outside the church only), and amplified noise went on till 3 a.m., and a free lunch was handed out at 6 a.m. It goes on for days. I could feel how knitted together the local people were. What are we to make of the birds? I doubt it is up to us. Like the fiesta, they are not put there for tourists.

But they cheered me up, and they seem far less of a superstition than the ravens at the Tower.

17 MAY 2003

A Lion Footrest

There's more to monumental brasses than rubbing 'em. The tendency is to take these medieval masterpieces for granted, for they are quite common in Britain. About 7,500 survive, half of them pictorial. On the Continent they are to be counted only in hundreds. As a boy I sometimes cycled over to Stoke d'Abernon in Surrey, where a fine brass of Sir John d'Abernon in chain-mail was made for his memorial in 1327. It was once thought to depict his father, and so to be the oldest brass depicting a knight in armour. The standard of its workmanship is remarkable.

Sir John has his feet supported by a lion – a small, stylized lion.

He and his footrest are included in *A Bestiary of Brass* (Heart of Albion Press), a compilation by an expert, Peter Heseltine, who shows how the animals are represented and explains their significance. The lion was said to sleep with its eyes open, signifying God's watchfulness over his people. While Sir John's lion is conventional in appearance, a dog on a brass for Sir Roger de Trumpington (1323), at Trumpington, Cambridge, is shown naturalistically with its tail up and chewing the end of the knight's sword-scabbard. Similarly, a pair of little dogs at the feet of Margaret Torryngton (1356), at Great Berkhamsted, Hertfordshire, are drawn with one curled asleep and the other sitting up alert.

A range of more exotic animals on brasses possess symbolic meanings of the kind recorded in bestiaries, the moralizing books so popular in the Middle Ages. The unicorn, which only permits itself to be captured in the lap of a pure virgin, was used as a symbol of the Incarnation; the pelican, which sheds its own blood to feed its young, was a symbol of Christ's saving sacrifice on the Cross. Those two symbols, familiar from medieval tapestries or from carvings in churches, are very ancient, being found in the book that seems to have started the convention of Christian bestiaries. It was known as the *Physiologus* and was apparently written, in Greek, in the second or third century. If, as references seem to indicate, it was known by Origen, who was born in 185, an early date seems certain.

The twelfth century saw a vogue for bestiaries, and by the fifteenth century they were being produced in the vernacular as well as Latin. William de Codrington, a Justice of the Common Pleas in the reign of Henry V, would have been literate in both. His feet rest on a panther, in a brass made in 1419 for the parish church at Gunby, Lincolnshire. The panther was distinguished from the leopard by having its spots singly rather than in groups of three. According to the bestiaries, the panther rests in his den after eating and falls asleep. After three days he wakes up and lets out a roar, at which all the other beasts gather round to smell his sweet breath. The dragon, however, will not come near, but hides in his hole, where he will sink into a torpor if the panther approaches. The panther is compared to Christ, who descended into hell and bound the great dragon, rising on the third day. Christ's sweet voice calls the faithful after his Resurrection.

A pelican surmounts the ornate gothic canopy engraved over the image of William Prestwyk, who died in 1436 at Warbleton, Surrey, where he had been rector since 1414. On the edge of the rector's cope, in black-letter script, is a Latin verse from the book of Job, familiar to us from Handel's *Messiah*, meaning: 'My redeemer lives, and on the last day I shall rise from the earth, and in my flesh I shall see God.' The pelican above is tending to its chicks in the nest, and a scroll reads '*Sic Xps dilexit nos*' – 'So Christ loved us.'

Heseltine also explains why tigers are shown with mirrors, why it is unlucky to kill red squirrels and how otters deal with crocodiles. It is just the sort of information you need once you have rolled back the protective bit of matting from an ancient brass and are puzzling over its fauna.

25 MARCH 2006

Elephant in the Tower

Two things that we assume about elephants – that they never forget and that they are afraid of mice – come from the medieval bestiaries, those written compilations of moralizing natural history that were popular for hundreds of years. I mention the elephant because, after writing here last week about animals on monumental brasses, I received a nice letter from a reader, Mrs Anne Willoughby, who asked if I had seen the fine elephant carved in wood on one of the misericords at Exeter Cathedral. A misericord is a little ledge on a choir-stall on which monks could lean while singing the Psalms. The misericord projects from the tip-up seats of the stalls, and the bracket supporting the ledge is often inventively carved.

There's a splendid cat playing a fiddle carved on a fourteenth-century misericord at Wells Cathedral. At Beverley Minster, one misericord shows a pair of woodwoses, or green men, bearing clubs and flanked by dragons. But Exeter has the oldest complete set of misericords in the country, carved in the third quarter of the thirteenth century. The unusual thing about the carved elephant is its naturalistic accuracy. Normally, medieval elephants are depicted fancifully. There is an elephant being strangled in the coils of a marvellous, elongated purple dragon with red wings in the so-called *Aberdeen Bestiary*, which was actually written and illustrated in England about 1200. If you have access to the Internet, you can find an image of it just by typing 'Aberdeen Bestiary' into your search engine. It is beautifully drawn, the elephant being pinkish and the two beasts standing against a brilliant background of gold leaf. The elephant has a trunk but no tusks, and is not what you expect to see in the wildlife park. Its ears are trefoils.

The Exeter wood carving has African elephantine ears and knees low down on its legs. This is important because, according to the sources on which bestiaries drew, the elephant has no leg joints, and sleeps leaning against a tree. Hunters in India were said to saw partly through a tree so that when the elephant leant on it, the beast would fall and be unable to get up again. When a fallen elephant trumpeted in alarm, the bestiary said, and its fellows gathered around, then neither 12 elephants together nor one great elephant could raise it from the ground, but only a small elephant using its trunk. This characteristic was moralized by the explanation that neither the old law nor the 12 prophets could raise a fallen sinner, but only the power of the meek and humble Christ.

But if the Exeter carving was not based on the usual sort of image in the bestiary, it might well have been inspired by the only drawing made by an Englishman of the thirteenth century who had seen an elephant. This was a monk of St Alban's Abbey, Matthew Paris (1200–59), an engaging figure, a gifted chronicler and artist and an endlessly interested observer. Matthew had seen the elephant sent by King Louis IX of France as a gift to King Henry III of England. It landed at Sandwich in 1255 and was kept in the king's menagerie in the Tower of London. 'We believe that this was the only elephant ever seen in England', Matthew wrote, and he drew it twice, once in a full-page drawing, tinted grey, with its keeper, 'Henricus de Flor', drawn in outline. In a study for this drawing, Matthew draws the trunk twice, articulated in different positions. He was clearly fascinated by the animal.

It is likely that the man who carved the Exeter misericord had seen Matthew's drawing, since St Alban's Abbey was a regular staging-post for travellers connected with ecclesiastical work. Henry III's elephant died in 1259, and in the same year so did Matthew Paris, at which point his *Chronicle* breaks off. But by great good fortune, the 130 drawings he included in its text survive.

1 APRIL 2006

Dogs Welcome

There's a woman who goes to my church and brings her dog with her. They come in briskly and quietly, and the dog, a good-sized Alsatian cross, curls up on the floor next to her. No one, I hope, minds. But when a friend of mine tried to carry her shih-tzu in her arms into the beautiful medieval church (once a monastery, founded from Cluny) at Paray-le-Monial in Burgundy, she got a *non-non* from the verger.

Former attitudes to dogs in church are a hotly disputed topic. Take the incident of the lightning at the parish church at Antony, Cornwall, in 1640. The bolt killed a dog 'at the feet of those who were kneeling in the chancel to receive the Sacrament', according to a contemporary source. Was that a sign that dogs were not welcome at such a solemn religious moment? Or was it merely a merciful providence that the worshippers were spared the dog's fate?

In a book that few but scholars will probably spend £50 to buy, *Sacred Space in Early Modern Europe* (edited by Will Coster and Andrew Spicer, Cambridge University Press), there is an interesting chapter by John Craig on the 'soundscape' of the English parish church in the sixteenth and seventeenth centuries. The sounds often included yelps, for Dr Craig says that dogs were 'invariably' present during services. One of the parish officers was the dog whipper, and his task was not to keep dogs out of church, but rather to keep them in order.

According to this interpretation of the evidence, Reformation-period dogs came in the same category as children whose 'walking, talking, crying or playing' so annoyed John Whitgift when he drew up an injunction for Worcester Cathedral in 1577. The status of canine churchgoing is the less clear because people did not always declare their motives openly. For example, Archbishop Laud (1573–1645) directed that railings should be put round the altar at the east end of the church. Now, this might be taken at face value as an anti-dog measure, judging by the evidence of Bishop Richard Montagu of Norwich (1575–1641), who directed that the railings round the altar should be 'close enough to keep out dogs from going in and profaning that holy place, from pissing against it, or worse'.

But as Dr Craig remarks, focusing on the control of dogs is 'at one level absurd, failing to take account of the theological and ceremonial ideas behind the Laudian altar policy'. Laud, as his contemporaries were well aware, held a high sacerdotal doctrine of the Eucharist, and all this talk of dogs was a red herring. At the bottom of Laud's idea of railing off the presbyterium, designating it as a holy of holies, lay a reversal of the earlier reformers' policy of bringing the 'table of the Lord's Supper' into the nave. By the same token, there were plenty of dogs wandering around during the most sacred moments in pre-Reformation times. There's a flop-eared little creature on the floor in *The Mass of St Hubert*, painted in about 1480 and now in the National Gallery, London. True, St Hubert was the patron of hunting, but this pooch couldn't have caught anything bigger than a mouse.

In France, the experience of the Moroccan traveller Ahmad ibn Qasim al-Hajari was quite different in the early seventeenth century from that of my spurned shih-tzu owner. 'When a worshipper has a dog or dogs,' he wrote, 'then they arrive at church before their owner and nobody sends them away.' In England, many parishes did appoint a dog whipper to keep order among the canine congregation. One of them features at the outdoor sermon at Paul's Cross, in the churchyard of St Paul's Cathedral, painted by John Gypkin in 1616 before the Fire of London destroyed cross and cathedral. The picture belongs to the Guildhall in the City of London.

Dog-tongs for the use of the parish dog whipper can still, I learn, be found at the churches of Clynnog Fawr, Gwynedd, of Llanynys, Denbighshire, and of Clodock, Herefordshire. I hope they will not be needed in my own parish.

10 JUNE 2006

Woodpecker's Dinner

Next to a picture of a clergyman in a cope admiring a hamster, the Rev. Professor Andrew Linzey has explained in the *Church Times* why he is in favour of church liturgies for the healing, blessing and burial of animals. Who could be against blessing pets? Oddly enough, some promoters of animal rights are, since they reject the keeping of animals as pets. That is not the attitude of Professor Linzey, an Oxford academic, who declares that 'for many, animals are the "significant others" in their lives'.

Professor Linzey has compiled a whole book of prayers for animals called *Animal Rites: Liturgies of Animal Care* (SCM Press). 'Holy Creator, we come together to thank you for the fellowship of other creatures, to celebrate their God-given lives, and to pray for compassionate hearts, so we may care for them and all creation' – that sort of prayer. Professor Linzey is not without a sense of humour. He tells the story of how, when he first held a service for animals, a man came to the altar rails clutching a ferret. As the eager young clergyman tried to administer a blessing, the ferret's owner exclaimed, 'No, don't touch it! It'll have yer f***ing finger off.'

But the question of the treatment of animals is a serious matter to the professor. 'In terms of pain, suffering and death,' he has written, 'what we do to millions of animals constitutes, I believe, one of the major moral issues of all time.' That is quite a claim. He does not, he argues, sell out to a postmodern secular sensibility, for blessings for animals are to be found in the *Rituale Romanum*, dating from 1614. That may be, but one can bless practically anything, from a bicycle to a battleship. I have seen photographs of packs of hounds being blessed. Who blesses the fox?

Professor Linzey has found a sermon by John Henry Newman from 1842, when he was a Church of England vicar, in which he says: 'Think then, my brethren, of your feelings at cruelty practised on brute animals, and you will gain one sort of feeling which the history of Christ's Cross and Passion ought to excite within you.' Newman's purpose was to encourage his English audience to sympathize with Jesus Christ; Professor Linzey takes it as an appeal to sympathize with animals. To him, they too are the object of 'God's absolute identification with the weak, the powerless and the vulnerable, but most of all with unprotected, undefended, innocent suffering'.

If one can see a certain danger of absurdity, it is nevertheless impossible to deny that God is deeply interested in his own creation. The anthropologist Mary Douglas has argued that the ritual prohibitions of the Old Testament were intended to point to God's universal lordship and loving care. Another thinker who has cut through much modern nonsense, Mary Midgley, argues strongly for the status of animals. Indulging in cruelty to animals is clearly wrong, but the alternative is not necessarily the establishment of a sort of universal welfare state for animals. Animals are different from men.

Recently I enjoyed the natural beauty of a pine forest in mountainous Spain. Unlike the British Forestry Commission's idea, this wood was full of life, notably of noisily woodpecking woodpeckers. If I were a woodpecker, I would be quite anxious about where my next meal was coming from, and be burdened with the responsibility of a nest at home full of beaks hungry for a delivery of bark insects. But the woodpeckers seemed perfectly happy and carefree, singing and drilling and flying away at a hint of an approaching hawk. Yes, animals are different from us, and what is good for the hawk is bad for the woodpecker. What is good for the woodpecker is bad for the bark insect. Certainly God is the Lord of all, but he is the Lord of life and death. Woodpeckers, even if they avoid the attentions of hawks, only live for so long. They aren't vegetarians, so why should I be?

9 OCTOBER 2004

8

Haphazard Hymns

Hashish-drunk

Nothing could be less likely than the origin of a hymn that is more popular than almost any other. (It has always figured in the top three each time the BBC has polled the three million viewers of *Songs of Praise* over the past 20 years.) I mean *Dear Lord and Father of Mankind* by John Greenleaf Whittier. Whittier (1807–92), an American Quaker, deeply disliked the singing of hymns in church. But an English Congregationalist, W. G. Horder, adapted one of Whittier's poems to make it a hymn in 1884, and there was not much Whittier could do about it. Stranger still are the bits of the poem left out. Entitled 'The Brewing of Soma', the poem dealt with various kinds of intoxication – by alcohol, drugs or fanaticism. Soma (a word later used by Aldous Huxley for the feel-good drug in *Brave New World*) was a sacred drink mentioned in ancient Sanskritic books of Indian religion. Whittier's poem is prefaced by a quotation from Max Müller, the first professor of philology at Oxford, who had misty racial theories based on these immemorial rites.

Eleven of Whittier's stanzas preceded the six retained for the hymn. They range over the Vedic hallucinogens, the dance of the Islamic dervish and the trance of the medieval Christian flagellant. How weird it would be if we sang to the familiar hymn-tune lines such as the following:

> The desert's hair-grown hermit sunk
> The saner brute below;
> The naked Santon, hashish-drunk,
> The cloister madness of the monk,
> The fakir's torture show!

As for the words that we do sing, it is hard to think of them without the melody that complements them so well. Yet in North America, the hymn is generally sung to a different tune, *Woodland*, by Nathaniel Gould. The British and Commonwealth melody, now called *Repton*, was the work of Sir Hubert Parry (1848–1918). It was originally written in 1887 for an aria, 'Long Since in Egypt's Pleasant Land', in his oratorio *Judith*. Only in 1924 did the director of music at Repton School fit it to Whittier's words.

I found the history of this hymn in the splendid new *Daily Telegraph Book of Hymns* (Continuum). It is edited by Ian Bradley, who really knows his onions. He is a reader at the University of St Andrews and a minister of the Church of Scotland, whose own hymn book he helped revise. The great feature of his new book is the introduction to each of the 150 chosen hymns. The stories are fascinating, and I kept turning from one to another well past my bedtime. The building up of a popular 'canon' of hymns has been very haphazard. Another hymn not widely sung until it found a winning tune is *All My Hope on God is Founded*. The words were by Robert Bridges, the champion of Gerard Manley Hopkins as a poet. Two decades before his own appointment as Poet Laureate, Bridges had acted as choirmaster in the Berkshire village of Yattendon, and in frustration at the poor quality of many hymns he compiled a new collection, published in 1899 as the *Yattendon Hymnal*. It included this hymn, based on one in German by Joachim Neander (1650–80), who provided a tune for it that is sometimes still used today. But it was only from 1930 that Bridges' translation gained popularity, thanks to a tune (called Michael) composed for it by Herbert Howells. Bridges also made a new translation of a medieval Latin hymn, *Salve mundi salutare*. It had already found a translator in Sir Henry Baker, who put it in the first edition of *Hymns Ancient and Modern* (1860). The version by Bridges begins 'O sacred head, sore wounded'. The tune, written for a German love song in about 1600, was taken by J. S. Bach and used five times in the *St Matthew Passion*, and what could be nobler and more moving?

12 NOVEMBER 2005

Bright or Wicked

In Barbara Pym's novel *No Fond Return of Love* (1961), Dulcie Mainwaring sings *All Things Bright and Beautiful* in a 'loud indignant voice', for she is waiting for the lines, 'The rich man in his castle,/The poor man at his gate,/God made them, high and lowly,/And ordered their estate.' But the verse has been omitted and she sits down feeling cheated of the indignation. In 1995, the late David Konstant, the go-ahead Catholic Bishop of Leeds, expressed his own indignation by calling the verse 'one of the most dreadful, even unintentionally wicked commentaries on society'.

The author of the hymn, Fanny Alexander (1818–95), intended it to bring to life for little children the clause in the Creed 'Maker of heaven and earth'. She also wrote *Once in Royal David's City* (for 'Born of the Virgin Mary') and *There Is a Green Hill Far Away* (for 'Crucified, dead and buried'). They were published in 1848 (when she was still Miss Humphreys) to raise funds for a school for the deaf. The book went through 100 editions.

Historically, the Church of England (or the Church of Ireland, to which Mrs Alexander belonged, being married to a man who became one of its primates) has favoured a stable social order. In the sixteenth century, it seemed obvious that every man had his natural master. In the *Book of Homilies*, which, as one of the 39 Articles explains, are 'to be read in churches by the ministers diligently and distinctly', we find this stirring sentence on earthly authority: 'Take away Kings, Princes, Rulers, Magistrates, Judges, and such estates of God's order, no man shall ride or goe by the high way unrobbed, no man shall sleepe in his owne house or bedde unkilled, no man shall keepe his wife, children, and possession in quietnesse, all things shall bee common, and there must needes follow all mischiefe, and utter destruction both of soules, bodies, goodes, and common wealthes.'

In the *Homilies* and in the Prayer Book, 'estate' and 'state' are used synonymously. The Prayer Book's short catechism, phrases from which used to remain with adults from their childhood instruction, declares that duty to my neighbour means: 'Not to covet nor desire other men's goods; but to learn and labour truly to get mine own living, and to do my duty in that state of life, unto which it shall please God to call me.'

Anthony Trollope misremembered the catechism answer, usually as 'that state of life to which it had pleased God to call him' (*Last Chronicle of Barset*; *The Eustace Diamonds*; *Lady Anna*; *Ayala's Angel*). In *Lady Anna* (1874), he returns to the question of social degree repeatedly, putting in the mouth of the old 'Keswick Poet' this creed: 'I believe but in one Lord, in Him who, in His wisdom and for His own purposes, made men of different degrees.' The Countess, mother of the heroine, berates her daughter: 'Do you not constantly pray to God to keep you in that state of life to which it has pleased Him to call you?' This is hardly what the catechism demands, especially as the girl is not covetous, but wants to marry beneath her. Later in the novel, Mrs Bluestone says: 'God Almighty has chosen that there should be different ranks to carry out His purposes, and we have His word to tell us that we should all do our duties in that state of life to which it has pleased Him to call us.' Here, Trollope as narrator remarks: 'The excellent lady was somewhat among the clouds in her theology, and apt to mingle the different sources of religious instruction.' As for Mrs Alexander's composition, it is important, as Ian Bradley, the editor of the *Daily Telegraph Book of Hymns*, points out, to notice the comma in 'God made them, high and lowly'.

The *New English Hymnal* has left out the offending verse at least since 1933. *All Things Bright and Beautiful* entered *Hymns Ancient and Modern* in 1904 and the satanic verse was not included even then.

'Most modern hymn book compilers omit the stanza,' wrote Maurice Frost in his *Historical Companion to Hymns Ancient and Modern*, 'though why rich and poor do not qualify as part of God's creation is never explained.'

8 JULY 2006

Jesus in the Womb

Why, asked my colleague Tom Utley, after the last *Telegraph* Christmas carol service, should anyone think God would abhor the Virgin's womb? He was referring to that line in *O come, all ye faithful* that goes 'Lo, he abhors not the Virgin's womb'. A good question, which I was quite unable to answer until this week, having read a book called *Redeemer in the Womb* by the theologian John Saward. I had put off reading it before, partly because I had assumed it was a nicey-nicey volume of a devotional 'pro-life' flavour. Goodness knows I detest abortion, but this book is not directly about that subject. Instead, it brilliantly explores what early writers in the Church thought about the months spent by Jesus in the womb of the Virgin Mary. A pagan presumption in the ancient world was that the female pudenda were indeed shameful, that women's insides were no better, and that women as a whole were second-rate. To this bundle of attitudes, a strand of heterodox thinkers, of a Gnostic, Manichaean, Docetist or otherwise flesh-hating tendency, added repulsion at the idea of God becoming incarnate in the messy entrails of a human being.

A third-century Neoplatonist called Porphyry of Tyre recoiled from the idea that 'the Divine entered the womb of the Virgin Mary, became a foetus, was born and wrapped in swaddling clothes, full of blood of the membrane, bile and other things'. By contrast, the good St Hilary (315–67), after whom the university Hilary term is named, while recognizing the popular distaste for things intestinal, is full of praises that God the Son, 'the invisible Image of God, did not scorn the shame that marks the beginnings of human life'. It is here that the phrase taken up by the unknown author of *O come, all ye faithful* comes in. I say the author is unknown, though it is certain that an eighteenth-century priest called John Wade wrote out the words; but the Latin original is not certainly his. Anyway that phrase is many centuries older, in the great hymn of praise, the *Te Deum*. 'Thou art the King of Glory, O Christ', it sings, as translated in the Book of Common Prayer. 'Thou art the everlasting Son of the Father. When thou tookest upon thee to deliver man, thou didst not abhor the Virgin's womb.' An earlier translation, from the fifteenth century, said, 'Thou horydest not the Virgin's womb.'

So the authors of these hymns rightly resisted the heretical suggestion that God did not become flesh in a real, human, uterine way. This is a point picked up by that delightful prose writer Lancelot Andrewes, in a sermon before King James for Christmas 1614. He knew St Hilary's words on the subject, and quoted them for the bookish king, in Latin and English. Christ as '*embryo*', says Andrewes, '*nostrae contumelias transcurrit*, the very contumelies of our nature, *transcurrit* is too quick a word, He "ran" through them; nay He stayed in them, in this first nine months'. You can almost hear him saying the words, which read as if taken down from his delivery.

Anyway, the upshot of the orthodox view of Jesus's life in the womb, from the time of the early Fathers, past that Jacobean Bishop Andrewes until modern times, when familiarity with old books in foreign tongues faded, is that the essential, salvific, atoning work of Jesus Christ, most obviously accomplished on the Cross, was begun in those months before birth, when he was as truly incarnated as afterwards. In the eastern Christian way of looking at things, mankind is made capable of becoming like God because God has assumed human flesh.

There is plenty more stimulating reading in Professor Saward's remarkable book. By chance, while I was reading it, I came across a fine polychromatic seventeenth-century statue of the Virgin with child – pregnant, that is. For the first time, I appreciated some of the insights that the sculptor of that statue would have shared.

19 MARCH 2005

The Bishops' Ban

A hundred years ago, the brand-new *English Hymnal* was announced in its own preface as 'a collection of the best hymns in the English language'. That did not stop the Archbishop of Canterbury in 1906 banning it. But the *English Hymnal* endured, and the present Archbishop of Canterbury says that it 'remains a triumph'. He writes about it in a foreword to a celebratory volume (the title of which, *Strengthen for Service*, is taken from a hymn enterprisingly translated from the Syro-Malabarese liturgy). The book is edited by Alan Luff and published by Canterbury Press.

Dr Rowan Williams should know, because as a boy the *English Hymnal* changed his life. Coming from a Presbyterian background, he found it fascinating when at the age of 11 he began to attend Anglican churches and sing in their choirs. 'Perhaps not everyone would think of the *EH* as a lively book', he admits, mentioning the 'hilariously dreary office hymns' it contains. Some people, he says, have 'complained about it as a monument to a particular sort of north London suburban tastefulness – the Edwardian ecclesiastical equivalent of sun-dried tomatoes in Islington'. But he rightly notes that 'it is given to few hymn books to be overseen by a composer of the stature of Vaughan Williams'.

The *EH* benefited from Ralph Vaughan Williams's original compositions and arrangements. Yet he was a strange choice as the musical editor of a new hymnal intended to enhance godly worship, for he was, from the end of his schooldays, fundamentally atheistical. Vaughan Williams, who gave two years of his time, was chosen by Percy Dearmer, the motor behind the new hymnal. Dearmer had already adopted the twin influences of Christian Socialism and the Arts and Crafts movement, as inspired by William Morris. His world had much in common with that of G. K. Chesterton (a hymn by whom was included in the *EH* in the year it was written).

Dearmer's first notable mark on the Church of England had been *The Parson's Handbook* (1899), a guide to church services as he liked to think they had been ordered in the Salisbury of the High Middle Ages. He championed dossals and riddel-posts as bulwarks against the decadence of the baroque. Anyway, when Dearmer came up with the idea of a hymn-book more Catholic than *Hymns Ancient and Modern*, part of his concept of musical beauty (and beauty for him was essential to worship) came from the tradition of musicologists like the folk-collector Cecil Sharp. It is curious to note the folk-songs that become hymn-tunes in the *EH*. There are *Tarry Trousers* ('Fight the good fight'); *The Bailiff's Daughter* ('When Christ was born in Bethlehem'); *The Royal George*

('Father hear the prayer we offer'); *The Unquiet Grave* ('The year is swiftly waning'); and *Stinson the Deserter* ('O God of earth and altar'). Of course, there is no more thought of the bailiff's daughter or tarry trousers when these hymns are sung than there would have been of the old song *L'homme armé* when Josquin Desprez's Mass setting was sung in the sixteenth century.

But it was not because of the music that the *English Hymnal* was seen as a scandal – rather because some of its hymns invited the intercession of saints. The Bishop of Oxford wrote to the publisher, Henry Frowde of the Oxford University Press, praising the book 'in binding and in printing' but adding that he made more 'serious criticism'. The Bishop of Bristol wrote: 'I cannot reconcile it to my conscience, or to my historical sense, to do less than prohibit a book which would impress upon the Church of England tendencies so dangerous.' He objected to the lines: 'For the faithful gone before us/May the Holy Virgin pray.' To this Dearmer retorted, 'Does the Bishop think we should sing, "May the Holy Virgin not pray"?'

The decisive blow came when the Archbishop of Canterbury expressed a strong wish that no church in his diocese should adopt the hymnal. The Oxford University Press saved the day with an edition ingeniously omitting five controversial hymns (Nos 185, 195, 208, 213 and 350), without leaving visible blanks or disturbing the numbering of the whole.

By an irony this compromise served so well diplomatically that the 'abridged' edition never gained wide sales, and surviving copies are scarce. All unaware of the row it caused, congregations today can sing the translation by Athelstan Riley (a member of the *EH*'s founding committee) of *Ave Maris Stella*: 'Jesu's tender Mother,/Make thy supplication/Unto him who chose thee/At his Incarnation.'

25 NOVEMBER 2006

9

Understanding Islam

Ramadan

We are in the midst of Ramadan, the Muslim holy month. Every-one knows this entails fasting, but how do Muslims in Britain actually observe it? I am not a Muslim, and trying to understand someone else's religion from the outside is like trying to join a conversation in a foreign language. It is easy to find from books that Ramadan is associated with a great event in the history of Islam, the beginning of the revelation of the Koran to the prophet Mohammed. The first verses were dictated by the angel Gabriel on the Night of Power.

To find out what Ramadan means in practice, I asked a young Muslim woman, Amina, who lives and works in London. For her it was a time to ask forgiveness and concentrate on religious matters. The day on which this lunar month is declared to begin depends on the moon's visibility, never a certainty in advance. Then, for 29 or 30 days, no food is to be taken or drink swallowed during daylight. For Amina, who still lives in the family home, Ramadan means getting up at five and eating before the sun rises at six, and, after the sun sets at about four, taking a meal to end the day's fast – traditionally of dates and milk. The complement to fasting (one of the five pillars of Islam) is prayer, another pillar. Before daybreak, the faithful Muslim makes a declaration that she intends to fast that day, and asks pardon for all her sins.

At any time of year, prayer five times a day is a Muslim obliga-tion. During Ramadan, the day begins with two short prayers, the *Faraz*, and two in the name of the prophet, the *Sunnat*. Prayers accompany standing, placing hands on knees and prostration, and then verses from the Koran are said, according to choice – more often short ones. The verses are recited in Arabic, though many people in Britain use prayer-books with Arabic on one page and English on the other. Some prayer-books give phonetic

117

transcriptions of the Arabic, so that verses may be said even when the believer cannot read Arabic. The use of the original Arabic is essential, since Muslims regard the Koran as verbally dictated by God. The 27th night of Ramadan, the very Night of Power, worth 1,000 other nights, demands prayer all night to gain forgiveness and ask God for what you want.

In Ramadan, visits to mosques are popular after sunset. For the *taraweeh*, the prayers said at about 7 p.m., Regent's Park mosque is packed. Women, of course, use a separate enclosure from the men. After the *taraweeh*, the family returns home for a large dinner (but not the lengthy feasting common in Saudi Arabia).

For Amina, refraining from going out socially or to the cinema in Ramadan brings her closer to contemporaries who are observing the same restrictions. And then there is always Eid-ul-Fitr to look forward to, the most enjoyable feast of the year, after a good month seeking God's mercy.

9 DECEMBER 2000

Ten Things to Know

It would be terrible to think that Muslims in Britain knew as little about non-Muslims as non-Muslims know about them. To explain Christianity in ten short points would be no easy task, but as a cut-out-and-keep *aide memoire*, here are ten things to know about Islam.

1. The five pillars of Islam
First: 'There is no god but God. Mohammed is the messenger of God.' Allah is the Arabic word for God. He is absolutely one, eternal, the Creator and Ruler. He is the Merciful. Ninety-nine names of God are to be found in the Koran. Second: Prayer five times a day, at dawn, midday, mid-afternoon, sunset and nightfall. Third: Almsgiving (*zakat*). Fourth: The fast of Ramadan. During this month no food or drink are taken during daylight hours. Fifth: The pilgrimage to Mecca, the hajj.

2. Sunni Islam

About 90 per cent of Muslims. There is no ruling hierarchy. Learned men, the *ulama*, decide on the right way to behave. Relations with God are strictly unmediated – imams and saints are not seen as intercessors. Two thirds of Muslims in Britain are Sunnis from the Indian subcontinent.

3. Shi'ite Islam

About 10 per cent of Muslims. Iran is dominated by Shi'ism. Since the killing of Husain, the grandson of Mohammed, in 680 at the battle of Karbala (in present-day Iraq), the Shi'ites have lived a largely persecuted existence, and they see Husain's death as part of a salvific penitential response to sin. They await the return of the Twelfth Imam in succession to Mohammed, who is expected as the Mahdi at the end of time to bring peace and healing to the world.

4. The Koran

This holy book was dictated by Mohammed. It is believed to be the uncreated word of God. So it may not be amended, and is studied in the original Arabic; translations are held to be paraphrases. The book in which it is written is treated with respect.

5. Mohammed (570–632)

The last prophet sent by God. Some Muslims say 'peace be upon him' after his name or write 'pbuh' or '*saaw*', the initials for Arabic words meaning the same. Mohammed is a human being; worship is of God alone.

6. Sharia

'God has not revealed himself and his nature, but rather his law', it is said. The Arabic for this law is sharia. It derives from the Koran and the customs (*sunnah*) of the prophet Mohammed, as set down in records of his behaviour, known as *hadith*. Early consensus on the law was known as *ijma*. There are four strands of Sunni Islam loyal to the four schools of law, named after the figures credited with founding them: the Hanafis, the Hanbalis, the Malikis and the Shafi'is. A set of punishments of great severity are known as *hadud* (singular *hadd*). These include stoning or lashing for unlawful sexual intercourse, lashing for drinking alcohol, and cutting off hands for theft. In practice these are not always imposed.

7. Mosques
These are places where the community pray. Those who enter should be ritually pure. There are no priests in Islam. A senior leads prayers. The people face the direction of Mecca. The imam, the cleric who leads prayers, delivers a sermon, at least on Fridays. This is the day for public worship, but work is not prohibited.

8. Mecca
The city where Mohammed was born. During the hajj, pilgrims walk round the Kabah, the cubic building rebuilt by Abraham, with a black stone built into one wall. The Kabah is covered with a black cloth out of reverence.

9. The hijab
A woman's enveloping dress. In Mohammed's time the word referred to the tent-divider behind which women would sit when men were present. The intention is modesty.

10. Jihad
The Arabic for struggle, its primary meaning is the interior struggle to do good and avoid evil. It also refers to war against enemies of Islam. Conditions for its use include authorization by the leading Muslim scholar in a state. Noncombatants, women and children are not to be killed. The terrorism we see now has been devised by political followers of radical Islam whose religion derives from the Wahhabi puritans of Arabia.

23 JULY 2005

The Sacrifice

Yesterday was the Muslim feast of Eid al-Adha. It is of some interest to consider it during the Christian season of preparation for Easter, the feast of the paschal sacrifice. For Eid al-Adha commemorates the sacrifice by Abraham of a sheep in the place of his son, whom he was willing to sacrifice if it had been God's will. In the Bible, that son was Isaac; in the Koran, his name is given as Ishmael. (This Eid is not to be confused with Eid al-Fitr, the feast at the end of the month of fasting of Ramadan.)

Eid al-Adha takes place on the tenth day of the month of the hajj. Since the Muslim calendar depends on the moon, the timing of the hajj varies from year to year. Muslims around the world on this day dress in their best clothes, go to the mosque for special prayers, hear a sermon and greet each other, usually in the formula 'Eid Mubarak' – blessed feast, happy holiday. It is a jolly day and children are given sweets. But the great link between all the world's Muslims and their brothers and sisters at Mina (near Mecca) on the hajj is the sacrifice of a sheep (a camel or cow may be killed, but this is more difficult and more expensive). Al-Adha means 'the sacrifice'.

The Muslim Council of Britain has posted on its website a handy list of 19 abattoirs that will make facilities available for proper slaughter this weekend (the sacrifice being valid during the three days following the day of Eid). It is not exactly ritual slaughter, for it is a spoken prayer and not a liturgical ceremony that renders the slaughter an acceptable sacrifice. Otherwise the ordinary provisions for making the meat halal are followed; blood is not allowed to remain in the carcass.

The general principle is that the sacrifice can be performed at this time by a Muslim man on behalf of himself and the members of his household, and he may apply the benefits to whomever he wishes, living or dead. A third of the meat is traditionally allocated for the family, a third as a gift to others and a third for the poor. It is worth realizing, if the idea of personally slaughtering an animal seems distasteful to a western mind, that the idea of sacrifice is deeply rooted in Jewish religious thought and in Christian theology. To a Muslim, the idea of Jesus offering himself in the Christian Eucharist can be far more alarming at first sight than the killing of a sheep seems to most Christians.

As Mary Douglas explains in her recent book *Leviticus as Literature*, sacrifice not only seals covenants between God and his people, but also identifies all creation as God's own. In the chapter of the Koran dedicated to the hajj, the 34th verse may be interpreted thus: 'And for every nation We have appointed religious ceremonies, that they may mention the Name of Allah over the beasts that He has given them for food. And your God is One God, so you must submit to Him Alone.'

23 FEBRUARY 2002

Scourged Shi'ites

The sight of hundreds of men beating their backs with chains and cutting their foreheads with knives is enough to frighten and disgust the standard western city-dweller. For many (of those who notice it among the population of Britain) the celebration by Shi'ite Muslims of Ashura might well remind them of a trailer for that film, *The Passion of the Christ*, about the sufferings of Jesus.

I certainly do not want to offend either group of believers, but some similarities have long been noticed between the street tableaux that mark the day of Ashura and those that are presented in many Spanish cities, for example, during Holy Week, representing the flagellation, the carrying of the Cross and the crucifixion of Jesus. The similarity is visually striking and conceptually intriguing. Ashura, the tenth day of the Islamic month of Muharram, was traditionally the day that Noah's Ark touched land. That is relevant, but the great event commemorated by millions of Shi'ites is the martyrdom in the year 680 (AH 61) of Husain (also spelled Hussein), the grandson of the prophet Mohammed, at Karbala, which is only as far from Baghdad as Oxford is from London.

Last year was the first for some time in which the Shi'ite majority in Iraq were able to celebrate Ashura with freedom, since Saddam Hussein's secularist regime repressed such public acts. Ashura is not just like Trafalgar Day, an historical anniversary.

The death of Husain is held by Shi'ites to have a universal redemptive value. I have seen it said that an incentive for taking part in the mourning rituals on this day is the belief that they are 'an aid to salvation on the Day of Judgement'. In a way, that is true. But there is also an explanation of the rites which is less like a penny-in-the-slot machine. Take the case of pagan rain dances. A generation of western anthropologists took them for a device to obtain rain and fertility. Such an idea, if it could be explained to a raindancer, would make him double up in laughter – for to him, the dance didn't cause the rain, it celebrated, and proleptically gave thanks for the rain.

Among believers, celebration of the sacrificial martyrdom of Husain would not produce salvation on the Day of Judgement. Really the believer is just recognizing a salvific fact not of his own making. Only the mercy of God can supply salvation, and if Husain's martyrdom is salvific, it is because God counts it as acceptable. The family into which Husain was born is sometimes likened by Shi'ite preachers to that Ark of Noah; indeed the similitude was attributed to a *hadith* or saying of Mohammed himself. Noah's Ark has always been used by Christians as an image of salvation.

As for Holy Week processions, only the most foolish Christian would think that carrying a float bearing a tableau of the scourging of Jesus is going to win the bearer salvation on Judgement Day. Rather, while undertaking a token suffering, the penitent in the procession is acknowledging the one meritorious sacrifice of Jesus, which transcends history and is applicable year by year. Obviously an Ulster Presbyterian is likely to find the Good Friday processions in Seville grotesquely superstitious. In a similar way a Wahhabi Muslim finds Shi'ite rites at Ashura shocking and blasphemous, and would stop them if he had the power.

There is another vein running through Shi'ite history. Just as Husain's companions in martyrdom were few and were deserted by the majority, so the Shi'ite community has found itself persecuted in successive centuries. This can produce a victim mentality borne in private, or, in some cases, extreme political reaction. Somehow some people can even convince themselves that suicide bombing is a kind of martyrdom.

28 FEBRUARY 2004

Saints' Shrines

Poor Iraq has a central place in the formation of Islamic spirituality, for it was at Karbala that Husain, the grandson of Mohammed, was killed, in AD 620. To Shi'a Muslims, the majority in Iraq, though only about ten per cent of the Islamic world, this martyrdom is a pattern of how the just man fares among the ungodly.

Husain was buried at Karbala and his remains venerated there, although Cairo and Damascus, among other places, claim to have his head. There is no single account of the role of saints in Islam. This should be no surprise to Christians, who would be hard put to explain consistently the part saints play in their own religion. Indeed it is largely the attitude of Protestants to saints that has made people find an analogy between Protestantism and Sunni Islam (and thus an analogy between Catholicism and Shi'a Islam). The comparison does not always enlighten.

According to Josef Meri of Berkeley University, an expert on the cult of saints in medieval Islam, the practice called *ziyara* – visiting the tombs of saints – was once ubiquitous. 'Tombs and shrines', he writes, 'were integrated into every aspect of daily life.' This was not, though, without controversy. The fierce medieval Islamic 'puritan' Ibn Taymiyyah (1263–1328) distinguished between lawful and heretical *ziyara*. 'In the legally permissible ziyara', he wrote, 'the living does not have need for the dead by making a request of him or seeking his intercession. But rather, the dead derives benefit from the living. God the Exalted has mercy upon the living who supplicates for the dead.' Although Ibn Taymiyyah cursed both Christians and Jews for their veneration of tombs, a seventeenth-century Christian puritan would have agreed with him that it was wrong to seek a dead saint's intercession with God. On the other hand, the Christian puritan would have abominated prayers for the dead, which all Muslims offer.

Ibn Taymiyyah was working in the tradition of Ibn Hanbal (died 855), the founder of the most 'puritanical' of the four great schools of interpretation of Islamic practice. Some of his followers identified *ziyara* as *shirk*, a fundamental compromising of God's sole provident status. Others resisted any such ban. In

Baghdad, Abu Hamid al-Ghazali (1058–1111) defended *ziyara*, though he forbade kissing or rubbing the tombs of loved ones or saints. These medieval debates are not forgotten today. The dominant Wahhabi sect in Saudi Arabia hates *ziyara*. In the twentieth century, domes or monuments at saints' tombs in Saudi Arabia were destroyed.

But in present-day Damascus it is possible to see pilgrims from Iran and central Asia making a *ziyara* to the many shrines of the family of the prophet Mohammed. And on Mount Carmel in Israel, the prophet Elijah is venerated by Christians, Jews and Muslims. All three monotheistic religions hold that God has performed wonderful works through men. How that is to be recognized is bitterly debated even among themselves.

25 JANUARY 2003

Presence of God

We don't know the simplest things about Islam, those of us who have not been brought up in it. I have just read an article on 'The Remembrance of God' by a learned Shi'a Muslim, Ayatollah Muhsin Araki. ('Ayatollah' is the title for an outstanding religious jurist. The article appears in a book, *Catholics and Shi'a in Dialogue*, Melisende.) He writes about what Christians think of as prayer. I am not trying to reduce Islamic teaching to Christian equivalents, for the point of listening to Muslims is to try to grasp their meaning of a term, and not twist it to a more familiar one.

The ayatollah is talking about *dhikr*, in Arabic. This refers both to bringing to mind God and to invoking him. This invocation of God brings peaceful virtues, and entails 'man's awareness of God's Lordship and his service of Him'.

The ayatollah presents a scheme of the stages of *dhikr*. There are three stages: with the tongue, with actions, and with the heart. For *dhikr*, there are five initial rules:

1. To turn to God, while turning the mind away from everything else.
2. Purity, of intention – seeking nothing but God's pleasure.
3. Entreaty and broken-heartedness (also called self-abasement and humility). The worshipper feels, as the Koran suggests, like those in danger at sea with no saviour except God. (One cannot help recalling Psalm 107: 'They go down again to the depths: their soul is melted because of trouble. They reel to and fro, and stagger like a drunken man, and are at their wits' end. Then they cry unto the Lord in their trouble.')
4. Fear and awe. Humans feel shame before God's justice on contemplating their failure to perform his will.
5. Abundance of invocation. The 'hypocrites' (bad men) 'are known for their lack of frequent invocation of God'.

So, with these five elements in place, we come to the:

First stage: invocation with the tongue. This is the proper recitation of ritual prayers (as directed daily in Islam) and of other, supererogatory, prayers.

Second stage: invocation with actions. Believers enjoin (and do) good acts. The Koran mentions regular prayers among these, and almsgiving.

Third stage: invocation with the heart. Any prayer entails movement of the heart, but this stage relates to a kind of transformation of the heart into 'radiance' or 'purity' (*safa*). It is easy to see parallels in classic Christian teaching on prayer.

The third stage may be divided into three again: a. invocation by state; b. invocation by quality; c. invocation by detachment and annihilation.

a. Invocation by state. This can be: 1. By wakefulness (or perhaps 'awakening'). Those who have fallen into the darkness of forgetfulness of God are illuminated by a flash of invocation. 2. By refraining. The invocation of God prevents sins. 3. By return – to God after sinning. 4. By vision – seeing God without the intervening veil of self.

b. Invocation by quality. This higher state entails a constant awareness of God and the seeing of all things in him. There are some beautiful Iranian poems, and one by Baba Tahir of Hamadan includes the lines:

When I look to the sea, the sea I see is you
When I look to the prairie, the prairie I see is you.

c. Invocation by detachment and annihilation. 'The invoker is transformed into the pure remembrance or invocation of God.' Another article in the book, by Reza Shah-Kazemi, points out that the believer is ideally 'at prayer' at all times. That is certainly the Christian teaching, too.

In explaining all the doctrine on *dhikr*, constant reference is naturally made to Mohammed. A popular prayer itself goes: 'O God, bless Mohammed and his descendants.' Christians, no matter how much they respect Mohammed, are unlikely to make him a constant theme of their prayer. For their part, the prayer of Muslims cannot be Trinitarian and Christocentric. The two religions are different.

3 SEPTEMBER 2005

An Old Game

The Government's attitude to Muslims shows dangerous signs of following that of the Roman Empire towards the early Christians. Tony Blair, before leaving for his mystery holiday destination, said threateningly that 'the rules of the game are changing'. There was a more specific suggestion that 'extremist' mosques would be closed down. Sir Ian Blair's police officers noting down suspect sermons in Bengali or Arabic is a pleasingly comic idea, even if their intention is not. Behind the unstable New Labour view of Islam is an implicit concept of good Muslims, Uncle Toms, like Sir Iqbal Sacranie or Dr Zaki Badawi, and bad Muslims, like whoever the week's 'preacher of hate' happens to be. The 'bad' Muslims are said to be fundamentalists, as if the 'good' Muslims did not really believe what the Koran says. The end not quite in view is of a new kind of Islam, reformed out of its obscurantist dogma.

The trouble is that the religion of Islam is at odds with the metropolitan presumptions of New Labour, which sees the hijab as oppressive to women and takes it for granted that abortion, homosexual partnerships and *The Satanic Verses* are goods to be defended by law and policy. Not only criminal acts against them are to be put down, but also aberrant opinions. 'Hate crime' elides into 'thought crime'. The early Christians were at odds with the presumptions of the empire. They boycotted the circus and would not sacrifice to the emperor. In the Roman polity, refusal of emperor-worship was not a matter of private religious opinion: it subverted the social structure by which imperial subjects were keyed loyally into the state. Like British Muslims, the early Christians were reluctant to fight in the army. When the pagan Celsus challenged the Christian philosopher Origen, in the middle of the third century, to say if Christians would fight if bidden by the emperor, he replied that they would help with their prayers, which would be 'a greater help than that which is given by soldiers'. The emperor could hardly have agreed.

Just as Muslims in Britain are accused of having more loyalty to their co-religionists than to their country, so the Christians of the first centuries annoyed their compatriots by pointing to another kingdom. In the second century, the magistrate who examined the aged Christian confessor Polycarp took pity on his years and urged him to swear by the spirit of Caesar and revile Christ. The old man replied: 'Fourscore and six years have I been his servant, and he hath done me no wrong. How then can I blaspheme my King who saved me?' This stance was clear from the first. 'Here we have no continuing city,' the Epistle to the Hebrews declared. 'We have no desire to take part in your public meetings,' said Tertullian in the second century. 'We acknowledge one all-embracing commonwealth – the world.'

To be sure, the early Christians did not make war on the Roman state, as radically politicized Islamists do on western countries, but the Roman authorities still tried to shut down 'extremist' Christian meeting-houses and confiscate their books. From the year 303, under the emperor Diocletian, there was a sys-tematic campaign to get Christians to hand over their books. Those who did were called by their fellow believers *traditores*, or traitors. Those who refused, and often met cruel deaths, were called martyrs, or witnesses.

Radical Islamists today are accused of loving death. 'It is a virtue to despise death,' wrote the Christian poet Lactantius in the early fourth century. 'Not that we seek death, or of our own accord inflict it upon ourselves.' But later in the same century, St Augustine of Hippo complained of heretical Christians who were so keen to attain martyrdom that they did indeed bring death on themselves.

Unlike the ancient Romans, modern liberals are unused to admitting that they think their own beliefs are right and those of alien religions must be put down. Their game is now changing.

20 AUGUST 2005

Intolerant Tolerance

I'm alarmed at what Mr David Bell, the chief inspector of schools, has been saying, not because of his opinions, to which he is entitled, but because he has the power to enforce them. He told Jeremy Paxman the other night that schools would be shut down if they didn't do what he told them. In a speech this week, Mr Bell previewed his official report, published next month. There he will draw attention to the growing number of independent 'faith' schools – about 100 Muslim schools educating 14,000 pupils, 50 Jewish schools educating 9,500 pupils and 100 evangelical Christian schools. 'Parents should be able to choose how their children are educated,' Mr Bell concedes. 'But faith should not be blind. I worry that many young people are being educated in faith, with little appreciation of their wider responsibilities and obligations to British society.'

Certainly, responsible citizenship is welcome, though I can't see much evidence of it from many state comprehensive pupils. But, since Mr Bell chose to focus on Muslim schools, what are we to make of this: 'Our common heritage as British citizens, equal under the law, should enable us to assert with confidence that we are intolerant of intolerance, illiberalism and attitudes and values that demean the place of certain sections of our community, be they women or people living in non-traditional relationships.' What does he mean, 'common heritage'? Ulster children haven't got a common heritage with Welsh children; second generation

Bengali immigrants haven't got a common heritage with Islington atheists. The law of the land applies to all, but the law doesn't yet entirely impose 'attitudes and values'.

And who are these people 'living in non-traditional relationships'? Does he mean British Buddhist monks, Mormons, Moonies? Probably not. He probably means 'lesbians and gay men' as the phrase has it. And although homosexuality is not unknown in the Muslim world, it is hardly treated with tolerance by Islamic state law or in Islamic religious teaching. The same goes for adultery, whether traditional or not. So if the only immutable moral law is that 'we are intolerant of intolerance', that might leave good Muslim schoolteachers in a bit of a pickle. And not just Muslims, for it depends on what you regard as intolerance.

Many parents like to send their children to church schools or 'faith' schools because there they receive a consistent moral education, not just in theory but also in how they are expected to behave. That morality derives from the religious ethos of the school. (It is very hard to work out a moral system from scratch; many humanists say they do it, but much of its content is taken second-hand from Judaeo-Christian antecedents.) Mr Bell demands that children be taught about faiths different from their own and about the beliefs of people who hold no faith. Fine, as long as that does not mean implying that their parents' beliefs and those of the school are no better than all the odd ideas of Muggletonians, Fifth Monarchy Men or worshippers of Odin.

Learning facts is not the same as being brought up in a religion. Muslims treat the physical book in which the Koran is written with great respect, not putting it on the floor, for example; British Christians don't treat it in the same way, but then, except in church worship, they merely shove their own Bibles on a shelf any old how, alongside *The Da Vinci Code*. A Muslim school would, I think, not tolerate such treatment of the holy Koran.

What about this? Last October the *Telegraph* reported the case of a Catholic teacher who was told her contract would not be renewed if she insisted on getting married in a civil ceremony. 'I am convinced that I was forced out because of my choice to marry outside of the Catholic Church,' she said. 'I am a Catholic but I have issues with the faith.'

It looks as if some faith schools are going to have 'issues' with Mr Bell.

22 JANUARY 2005

Not So Sunny

In Cordoba, amid the souvenir shops in the former Jewish quarter where the streets are too narrow for the horse-drawn tourist carriages, stands a statue of Moses Maimonides. He lived from 1135 to 1204, so we have just completed a year's celebrations of his 800th anniversary.

The impression taken away by the careless tourist is that in Maimonides' day, under Muslim rule, the culture of Cordoba blossomed under the palm trees in an atmosphere of benign religious tolerance.

It was not so simple, for at the age of 13 Maimonides (known to the Jews of his day as Moses ben Maimon) fled with his family from Cordoba when it came under the rule of the Almohads, who cracked down on both Judaism and Christianity. Christians and Jews had lived under Muslim rule since 711. They had to pay a special tax and to wear special signs on their clothes. Children of marriages to Muslims had to be reared as Muslims. In the ninth century came a string of Christian martyrs in Cordoba, some rather rash, such as St Rogellus, who entered the crowded mosque to preach Christ.

In 929 Cordoba and its territory was declared an independent caliphate under Abd-ar-Rahman III. His clan, the Ummayads, originated in Mecca, and ruled as caliphs in Damascus from 661 to 750, being then overthrown by the Abbasids. The Umayyads set up an independent emirate in Spain in 755. An emirate or kingdom was one thing, a caliphate like that in Cordoba was quite another, for there was meant to be one caliph for all Islam. Abd-ar-Rahman gave Christians important positions. Under his rule and that of his bibliophile son, Cordoba flourished as a centre of learning. But afterwards came constant power struggles, and by 1016 the caliphate had collapsed. It was no gentle climate in Cordoba a century later when Moses Maimonides' family escaped. Nor did Maimonides' contemporary and fellow physician in Cordoba, Ibn Rushd (1126–98) find it easy. Ibn Rushd, known to western philosophy as Averroes, was himself banished because, though a Muslim, he was a philosopher.

Maimonides and Averroes had things in common, as indeed they had with Thomas Aquinas (1225–74), who was influenced by both. First they took the thought of Aristotle seriously. Aristotle had been rediscovered by the West through a long chain of transmission. His work had been translated by Christians into Syriac in Mesopotamia and then into Arabic, which is how it was known to Averroes and Maimonides (who wrote in Arabic). It was translated again into Latin by scholars at various geographical meeting points of cultures. Secondly, Maimonides was a rationalizer. His best-known work, the *Guide for the Perplexed*, was intended to provide a reasonable approach for the study of Scripture. Maimonides was condemned by some strict religious lawyers and also by mystical Cabbalists, who managed to mark his tomb as that of a 'heretic'.

Averroes also tried to write about God rationally. He has been unfairly accused of believing in a system of double truth – saying one thing in religion and another in philosophy. He meant to defend Islam, but his ideas were far more influential on Christian philosophy than on Islamic ideas. It is worth realizing that by praising the philosophy of Averroes you will not please a modern Wahhabi (a hardline Muslim believer of the Saudi Arabian school, the stance of which has informed politically radical Islamism, including the sympathizers of al-Qa'eda). Wahhabis take their cue from Ibn Taymiyyah (1263–1328), who insisted that it was culpable to speculate beyond what is said about God in the uncreated Koran.

In his writings, Aquinas respectfully refers to Maimonides as Rabbi Moses and to Averroes as The Commentator. In a fresco in Santa Maria Novella, Florence, Averroes is shown sitting at Aquinas's feet, but not in a conventional pose of vanquishment. He looks thoughtful.

1 JANUARY 2005

Abraham's Religion

A Jew was at church on Sunday. Of course any number of Jews might be present Sunday by Sunday, and no one would know, since Jews look like anyone else. But this man, wanting to show he too cared about the bomb atrocities in London, dressed in his prayer-shawl and phylactery, and prayed quietly on one side while we Christians went on with our morning Eucharist. His was a brave gesture and one that could not fail to be moving. Observant Jews do not like even to seem to join in the religious rites of Christians. If I put myself in the position of a Jew witnessing a Communion service, I can imagine experiencing feelings of revulsion at a ritual centred on a man who claimed to be God and whose death by crucifixion is said to reconcile God and mankind in a way that no sacrifices in the Temple of old did.

One might imagine that Muslims would feel more in common with Jews, since both religions believe in the God of Abraham, a transcendent God, one, holy, almighty, just and merciful. In fact Muslims blame Jews for allowing true religion to stray from its pristine Abrahamic purity. The account of 'salvation history' in the Koran contradicts the version of the Jewish Bible, which Christians call the Old Testament. And if Jews might find Christian worship uncomfortable, Muslims judge Christians to be guilty of *shirk*, the crime of associating created beings with God. Even though classical Christian theology defends the oneness of God quite as strongly as Muslim teaching, Muslims cannot understand how this is compatible with belief in three persons in the one God. They certainly reject indignantly any idea of Jesus being the Son of God, and, although they hold him a prophet, they deny he died on the Cross.

Why am I pointing out these incompatibilities between the three monotheistic religions? Because I cannot see how there can be understanding between Jewish, Christian and Muslim believers unless they know where believers of another religion stand. People who assert that these religions 'really' believe the same things have simply misunderstood the reality. Real differences in belief have consequences for any attempt at joint worship. It is good for Muslims and Christians to be friends and cooperate in running civil society. It is moving if representatives of Jewish,

Christian and Muslim communities stand in the street and pray to God. But these prayers are scarcely joint action; they are more like the proximity talks that negotiators like to arrange. Christians can speak directly to God in prayer, but their habit is to speak to God the Father through Jesus Christ, a practice unacceptable to Jews and Muslims. From the West, the great mistake is to suppose that if Muslims can be persuaded to conform to the customs of capitalist society, it will cut the ground from beneath the feet of the radical Islamists who promote violent action. The reverse is the case. Radical Islam has thriven in societies that were being opened up to western secular values, along with capitalist investment (usury in Islamic eyes), immodesty, alcohol and television. In the radicals' analysis these are manifestations of a new unholiness, of paganized ignorance or *jahiliyah*. Egypt, for example, was blamed for embracing these un-Islamic ways and avoided an Islamist revolution only by fierce repression.

To the politically radicalized Muslim, any country that does not operate under sharia, the godly law, belongs to the Dar al-Harb, the 'abode of war'. The traditional conditions for attacking the Dar al-Harb are no longer observed by the radical Islamists, and we see the results. Sunni Islam is not a hierarchical religion with leaders in authority, and there are no bishop-like leaders to blame. Radical politicized Islamists have a 60-year start on us in developing violent action, and are not to be won over by the offer of democracy, which they loathe, or invitations to joint prayer meetings.

16 JULY 2005

10

Brain Waves

God Is

In the current *New Yorker*, the novelist John Updike has some things to say about a new translation of the first five books of the Bible by Robert Alter (*The Five Books of Moses*, Norton). I can't say that I much care for Professor Alter's style, and it is not easy to see the point of another translation. But what made me sit up in Mr Updike's review was his astonishing conclusion 'that to the ancient Hebrews God was simply a word for what was: a universe often beautiful and gracious but also implacable and unfathomable'. Thus, at an imaginative stroke, the novelist undoes the great triumph of Judaic theology: the intuition of the one, immaterial, transcendent God. If Moses had been walking past as Mr Updike was typing, he might have felt like heaving a large stone at him.

Mr Updike quite properly focuses on one verse of Exodus – verse 14 in chapter three, which comes just after Moses sees the burning bush. It is a fantastic revelation, but to appreciate its impact requires a bit of spadework. 'God said unto Moses, I AM THAT I AM: and he said, Thus shalt thou say unto the children of Israel, I AM hath sent me.' That is the translation of the Authorized Version (1611). It breaks out into capital letters, just as it regularly puts the LORD in capitals, because both represent what is taken to be God's name.

Those words I AM THAT I AM are in Hebrew *'ehyeh 'asher 'ehyeh*. *'Ehyeh* is the first person singular of the Hebrew verb to be. The third person singular ('He is') is Yahweh. (A few hundred years ago this was mistranscribed as Jehovah.) When God tells Moses to refer to him, God uses the word Yahweh, and indeed the Douai translation of the Bible (1609) renders the sentence: 'Thus shalt thou say to the children of Israel, HE WHO IS hath sent me.' The Hebrew *'ehyeh 'asher 'ehyeh* would ordinarily be taken to mean 'I am what I am'. But a century or so before the time of Christ, the Bible was translated by Jews into Greek for the benefit of Greek-speaking Jews in the diaspora. This translation is known as the Septuagint. It translated *'ehyeh 'asher 'ehyeh* as 'I am the being', or 'I am the existing one' (in Greek: *Ego eimi ho on*).

This translation was extremely influential. The Jewish philosopher Philo of Alexandria, a contemporary of Jesus, in his *Life of Moses* (I, 75), glosses the verse from Exodus as an explanation from God of the self-designation he has chosen: 'There is no name whatever that can be properly assigned to me, who am the only being to whom existence belongs.'

Meanwhile Christians were spreading throughout the Roman world, and by the fourth century needed a reliable translation of the Bible into Latin. The learned Jerome based his translation of Exodus directly on the Hebrew version, not the Greek of the Septuagint, and his version of God's self-description was EGO SUM QUI SUM – 'I am who am'. This was to be the familiar translation of the verse in Exodus until the seventeenth century and beyond. It informed the piety and preaching of the clergy of Christendom. The phrase proved the perfect bridge between the God of the Bible and the God of philosophy.

Aristotle had called God the unmoved mover, the first cause. Jews and Christians knew him as the creator, bringing into being all things. The high point of Christian rational theology, at least in its aims and presumed achievement, came in the thirteenth century with the metaphysical analyses of Thomas Aquinas (who was familiar with Philo, among others). To him it was clear that God's essence was identical with his very being: as pure, burning act. Whatever Moses thought when he handed on the name, to the Christian philosophers it was obvious that this was a divine revelation of God as *ipsum esse subsistens* – subsistent being. As such, God is transcendent – not part or the sum of the universe of things – and all that exists owes its being to him.

6 NOVEMBER 2004

Doubts of Chauntecleer

In Evelyn Waugh's novel *Decline and Fall*, the clergyman Mr Prendergast explains his doubts to his fellow schoolmaster: 'I couldn't understand why God had made the world at all. You see how fundamental that is. Once granted the first step I can see everything else follows – Tower of Babel, Babylonian Captivity, Incarnation, Church, bishops, incense, everything – but what I couldn't see, and what I can't see now is why did it all begin?' A similarly fundamental doubt occurred to Anthony Kenny in 1963 and compelled him to leave the Catholic priesthood. Poor old Prendy ends up with his head sawn off in prison. Anthony Kenny, by contrast, became master of Balliol and has 40 books and a knighthood to his name. The latest is *The Unknown God*, subtitled *Agnostic Essays* (Continuum).

The word 'agnostic' was invented by T. H. Huxley at the end of the 1860s. It was eagerly adopted soon afterwards by Leslie Stephen, the father of Virginia Woolf, who found himself unable to continue assenting to the articles of religion to which he had signed up as a priest in the Church of England. After a similar crisis, Anthony Kenny has remained remarkably faithful to his fundamental doubt since the day 40 years ago that he found himself an agnostic of a particular kind. He does not use the label as a polite version of 'atheist'. In 1963, he identified his intellectual position as that of someone who does not know any way to justify rationally the faith in God he once held, but does not rule out the possibility that such a rationale might be found.

It is unusual for such a dogmatic objection to propel a man from the priesthood. A lot of Catholic priests left because they wanted to marry, and although Anthony Kenny later married, that was not his motive for seeking 'laicization'. True enough, the young Fr Kenny had also run into difficulties when he opposed nuclear arms as a clergyman. But the clincher was rather an odd intellectual problem. If God, he thought, is all-knowing then he knows about future evil doing by men. Yet this makes him responsible for it, since he is the cause of all – the very explanation of his omniscience. Therefore he cannot be the God taught in Christian doctrine.

I must say that when I get ideas like that I merely assume I've made a mistake somewhere, just as I do in adding up a lot of figures. Anthony Kenny was made of sterner stuff.

When he hospitably gave me a long interview last week he did mention that he had subsequently found that something like his own difficulty had occurred to many thinkers in the Middle Ages, who made the best job of countering it that they could. That I can believe, for, as every schoolboy knows, Chaucer makes comic capital out of learnedly citing Augustine, Boethius and Brad-wardine's views about divine foreknowledge in the context of the farmyard fate of Chauntecleer the cock.

Sir Anthony Kenny has beefed up his own arguments against God over the years. He asserts that since God, with no human tendencies or history, is completely alien to creatures such as us, then even if he existed he might not care much about our wellbeing. This seems to me worse than the worst hellfire preaching of a Calvinist such as Jonathan Edwards, who likened a sinful man to a spider that God is ready to chuck from the coal-shovel into the fire. To Kenny, extinction at death, about which he has no agnostic doubts, is far kinder than traditional Christian teaching on the reality of hell. Yet, if I have understood his position rightly, the kind of God that Kenny thinks possible – if not extant – is no better than a demiurge or satanic power. Such a Sauron-like god would be worth opposing even in a hopeless Promethean struggle. Only a God transcendently true and good in himself – a concept that Kenny declares illusory – is to be trusted and obeyed.

21 FEBRUARY 2004

Non-negotiable

It is the 450th anniversary of the birth of Richard Hooker this year – not that this is in reality any more significant than the 449th. Still, not only was Hooker's an extraordinary mind, but the things it worked out have importance today, or so Rowan Williams, the Archbishop of Canterbury, suggests in a new book. Eight essays by Dr Williams have been put together in *Anglican Identities* (Darton, Longman and Todd), and two of them are on Hooker. When short extracts from the book appeared in a newspaper recently, an academic friend of mine said reading them was like trying to grab hold of jelly in a bath. The newspaper might have done better to print one complete essay instead of bits and pieces, because the essay on Hooker, 'Philosopher, Anglican, Contemporary', is not at all slippery or spongiform.

Hooker's big book, credited with delineating an Anglican identity in opposition to Puritanism on one side and Papistry on the other, was called *The Laws of Ecclesiastical Polity*. Dr Williams asks why, if laws of Church discipline are changeable, doctrine is not. First it is necessary to decide what is meant by God's laws. Hooker enunciates a rule: 'The being of God is a kind of law to his working.' What does that mean? Well, some people in Hooker's time believed that God exercised his will in an arbitrary way, and that we had to put up with it and obey. Hooker asserts that God acts according to his nature. And God is good. 'To say that this diminishes the divine freedom,' Dr Williams comments, 'is to misunderstand the issue: God freely consents to the limits set to divine action by divine nature.'

I'm not sure I'd put it quite like that, but it is certainly the case that we can trust God's promises, which we would not be able to do if his acts were arbitrarily free. But because God is good, and acts in accordance with his goodness, and has the power, moreover, to do whatever he decides to, we can be sure he will keep his promises. That is good news, since we depend on them utterly. Hooker also points out that the goal of human beings, unlike the goal of other creatures, is not just 'good for us' but also 'good as such'. Human beings grow, or can grow, closer to this ultimate good. Therefore 'forensic justification will not do' for Hooker, Dr Williams says, 'because it can of itself give no useful account of spiritual growth'. So Hooker's 'classical concept of faith as a virtue or habit instantly puts him at odds with the mainstream of Reformed thinking'. Anyway, if God, the 'good as such', is our goal, then the disciplinary laws of the Church should be conducive to that end. There are some things which are so basic to human nature (as set up by God) that they cannot be changed; they are, in Dr Williams's language 'a matter of basic and non-negotiable procedure for being human before the creator'. Or as Hooker formulates it: 'Laws natural do always bind.' The only difficulty is correctly discerning these natural moral laws.

A Church in Hooker's system is a kind of society, and its laws should be for something; they should tend towards God's good, but not arbitrary, will. 'The Church', Hooker says, 'hath always power, as occasion requireth, no less to ordain that which never was than to ratify what hath been before.' In Dr Williams's formulation, 'true conformity to unchanging divine wisdom . . . requires a flexibility in discipline and polity that is impossible for the positivist and the primitivist.'

If that is true of discipline, why not of doctrine? In brief, because 'It is not up to us to "choose" our final ends, because we do not choose our nature', says Dr Williams. 'If we treat our doctrinal language as revisable in the same sense as our talk about polity, we risk treating our human ends as negotiable.'

24 JANUARY 2004

Sharing a Couch

Carl Jung, the psychoanalyst, had few close friends as he grew older, but one of them was an English priest who wrote to him out of the blue in 1945 proposing a reconciliation of theology and analytical psychology. 'The task before us is gigantic,' wrote the Dominican priest, Fr Victor White. This use of 'us' was reminiscent, notes Jung's biographer Ronald Hayman, of Jung's own confident approach to Freud years before.

Despite writing two careful books on Jungian psychology and sticking his neck out at a time when the Church hierarchy was deeply suspicious of psychoanalysis, White could not go far enough for Jung. Jung wanted to 'build up the symbol of the perfect contradiction in God by adding the darkness to the *lumen de lumine*'. White's response was that darkness, in the sense of evil, was a privation: one could talk about light without mentioning darkness, but not about darkness except in terms of light. Satan and Christ were certainly not counterparts. The most comical demand from Jung was for White to add a fourth member to the Holy Trinity of God the Father, Son and Holy Ghost – as if the teachings of Christianity were at the command of one middle-aged priest from Oxford, even in the unlikely event that he thought they should be changed so radically.

But there remains some point in the dialogue between psychoanalysis and religion – certainly for anyone with a foot in both camps. And now an even more ambitious call for reconciliation comes from the brilliant professor of philosophy at Reading, John Cottingham. I've been telling everyone enthusiastically about his new book, *The Spiritual Dimension* (Cambridge University Press), not because I agree with everything in it, but because it so compellingly articulates matters of the first importance, such as this. Professor Cottingham wants to heal the triangle of hostility between British (analytic) philosophy, religion and psychoanalysis. It follows from his consideration of religion not as a bare set of doctrines but as a practical living system in which the whole person takes part.

If philosophers were suspicious of Freud's ambitious systematizations, that was nothing compared with Freud's inimical identification of religion with immature neurosis. Freud's subtitle for his book *Totem and Taboo* (1913) was *Some Points of Agreement between the Mental Lives of Savages and Neurotics*. The supposed agreement was in their 'magical' attitude – the hoped-for 'omnipotence of thought' that Freud's famous Rat Man saw in his rituals, so that if he swore at a stranger that man might die. As for 'savages', anthropology has come a long way from the armchair speculations of Freud's contemporary James Frazer. The nearest Frazer had come to fieldwork was being taken as a child to see the Wild Man of Borneo at the fair by his nurse. The adult Frazer was so shocked by the contents of *Totem and Taboo* when Freud sent him a copy that he could not bring himself to acknowledge it, and years later referred to Freud as 'that creature'.

This is not at all the focus of Professor Cottingham's book. He regards Freud's work as a continuation of the insights of novelists, playwrights and poets. At the same time, he sets out to show that religion is no 'magical' mechanism or infantile longing for a father figure. Quoting Karl Rahner, he sees that surrender to God can produce 'a person who is really good to someone from whom no echo of understanding and thankfulness is heard in reply, whose goodness is not even repaid by the feeling of having been selfless'. Professor Cottingham also invokes the 'symbolic' aspect of religion (which he later detects in the rich connotations of the seemingly simple phrase in the Lord's Prayer 'Give us this day our daily bread'). For him, psychoanalysis is a deeply moral project, of the kind that Augustine attempted, as outlined in his *Confessions.* It is a question of integrating morality into the uncompartmentalized self. Again quoting Rahner, he opposes Freud's notion that man comes of age when religion is outgrown. 'The absolute death of the word "God"', Rahner wrote, 'would be the signal, no longer heard by anyone, that man himself had died.'

21 January 2006

Trinity in Mind

Thomas Aquinas (1225–74) is a surprisingly sympathetic writer for many Anglicans. For one thing, his work is saturated with an understanding of the early Church Fathers, as is the writing of seventeenth-century Anglican divines like Lancelot Andrewes or Jeremy Taylor. John Henry Newman, at the peak of his energies as an Anglican, had organized a joint translation by a team of scholars of the *Catena Aurea,* a collection made by Thomas Aquinas of patristic texts on the Gospels. But most of Thomas's work remained untranslated until the twentieth century.

A characteristic of Thomas is his reliance on the central role of the Bible in communicating faith. For Thomas, every book of the Old Testament is prophetic, benefiting from the *lumen propheticum,* the prophetic light, that brings with it certainty for truths unreachable by unaided human reason. Not that Thomas despised natural reason. He is famous for presenting five 'ways' by which the existence of God may be shown by reason alone, without depending on divine revelation. But in addition to the human mind working upwards to God, Thomas made use in his theology of downward reasoning, from the truths that God had revealed. An example of this is consideration of the Trinity: God the Father, Son and Holy Spirit. Since the Scriptures (Genesis) make it known that man is made in the 'image and likeness of God', might not a likeness of God's Trinitarian character be discerned in human nature?

In the so-called 'Penny Catechism' of the Catholic Church in England, children are, or were, taught that their likeness to God was chiefly in their souls, and in particular that the Trinity was reflected by the memory, the understanding and the will. This opinion was attributed to St Augustine. Certainly it makes sense to see the Holy Spirit as the Love (the loving will) of the Father and the Son, and the Son as the understanding of the Father. But it was not clear to me why the memory should have anything to tell us about God the Father. I found a clue this week. I found it in a new book by the scholar Aidan Nichols called *Discovering Aquinas* (Darton, Longman and Todd). In passing, he explained that, for Augustine, memory in human activity indicated the presence of God. It is not just memory in the sense of remembering where you have put the car keys. Memory is what understanding and will work upon for the mind to function. There is plenty about this in Book Ten of Augustine's discursive work *On the Trinity*.

At the same time, Augustine remained so impressed by the unknowability of God that he admits at one point that we call the Trinity in God 'persons' '*ne omnino taceretur*', 'lest otherwise we should fall silent'. Nevertheless theologians have said useful things since Augustine. And because Christians are meant to share the very life of the Trinity this is to them an interesting matter. Thomas Aquinas is a good place to seek insights.

31 AUGUST 2002

Trusting the Tongue

It is pleasant, as war once again grips the world, to find Sir Anthony Kenny, the former master of Balliol and distinguished philosopher, troubling at the age of 70 to take on a new generation of fashionable thinkers. Two proponents of the school of philosophy known as Radical Orthodoxy, John Milbank and Catherine Pickstock (the author of *After Writing*), have brought out a book called *Truth in Aquinas* (Routledge). Sir Anthony knows a good deal about Aquinas. The remarkable thesis of *Truth in Aquinas* is that only belief in transubstantiation can make sense of the world as interpreted by post-modernist eyes. Or perhaps one should say 'post-modernist tongues', since that is the organ upon which Sir Anthony concentrates, in a dissection of the book in *The Times Literary Supplement*.

The eccentric line of argument followed by Milbank and Pickstock is that Thomas Aquinas singles out touch among the five external senses as the most powerful. And, since the tongue comes into contact with the consecrated host at Holy Communion, it is the tongue that somehow tastes God directly. That would certainly have surprised Aquinas, who was hard to provoke. The nearest he ever came to a sharp word was when he remarked that the theologian David of Dinant '*stultissime*' – most foolishly – argued that God was prime matter. Milbank and Pickstock seem to have picked up a similar banner of perversity.

For Aquinas's understanding of the Eucharist was that bread and wine were turned into a different substance – the Body and Blood of Jesus Christ – in a change called transubstantiation. The appearances of bread and wine remained, along with the other 'accidents', including the taste and feel. So when the tongue sensed a taste of bread, it was not the taste of Christ, man and God, but a surviving accident of the bread that was there before being transubstantiated. Sir Anthony does not find comforting the Radical Orthodox suggestion that the whole world is like that – substances present under misleading appearances. This would mean, he says, 'that the socks I am wearing may, for all I know, be Queen Victoria transubstantiated'.

As a coda on a poetical level, one might point out that in the hymn attributed to Aquinas, the *Adore Te Devote*, the senses of touch and taste are singled out for their unreliability in detecting the presence of God in the Eucharist. '*Visus, tactus, gustus in te fallitur*', sight, touch and taste, he writes, are mistaken about you, '*Sed auditu solo tuto creditur*', but hearing alone is to be safely believed. He does not mean that hearing detects God in the sound of the host being broken. It is by believing what one has heard from God's revelation that sure knowledge comes – nothing, Aquinas writes, is truer than the truth of the Word of God.

10 NOVEMBER 2001

Fundamental Foundations

'Without saying as much in so many words, fundamentalism actually invites people to a kind of intellectual suicide.' Such a judgement would be unremarkable in the letters page of the *Independent*, perhaps. It is more surprising in a document for which Cardinal Joseph Ratzinger was responsible before he was elected as Pope Benedict XVI. After all, Ratzinger has sometimes himself been called a 'fundamentalist', usually by people who would be hard put to define the word. In a document called 'The Interpretation of the Bible in the Church', which Cardinal Ratzinger presented to Pope John Paul II in 1993, a whole section is devoted to fundamentalism.

The document (compiled by the Pontifical Biblical Commission) notes that the word fundamentalist is connected directly with the American Biblical Congress held at Niagara, in New York State, in 1895. There, conservative Protestant exegetes defined 'five points of fundamentalism'. These were: the verbal inerrancy of Scripture, the divinity of Christ, his virginal birth, the doctrine of vicarious expiation and the bodily resurrection at the time of the second coming of Christ. As far as the contents of the five points goes, 'The Interpretation of the Bible' has no quarrel with the fundamentalists. Ratzinger's colleagues objected rather that the 'way of presenting these truths is rooted in an ideology which is not biblical, whatever the proponents of this approach might say'.

The problem, they say, is that fundamentalism 'refuses to admit that the inspired word of God has been expressed in human language and that this word has been expressed, under divine inspiration, by human authors possessed of limited capacities and resources. For this reason, it tends to treat the biblical text as if it had been dictated word for word by the Spirit.' Now, this might sound very unfair – for, after all, the Catholic Church itself has said things like: 'Sacred Scripture is the speech of God as it is put down in writing under the breath of the Holy Spirit.' That sentence comes not from some medieval document, but from a dogmatic constitution of the Second Vatican Council published in 1965. In medieval manuscripts, the same idea is conveyed by miniaturists who show the dove of the Holy Spirit perching by the ear of the Gospel writers. But the document from 1993 is making the point that, while the Bible is inerrant because it comes from God, it has to be read according to human conventions of speech.

In any case, I do not hope to give a thorough account of fundamentalism here. It is just worth noting that it is not a synonym for 'dogmatic' or 'old-fashioned'. Ratzinger's attitude to the Bible was what most strongly struck me when I read an unusual book on him, or rather on him as the new Pope. It is *Benedict XVI* by Laurence Paul Hemming (Continuum). It is hardly a conventional biography – you won't find out much about his love of cats or his favourite sausage. Laurence Paul Hemming is dean of research at Heythrop College, London University, and his book surveys in a fairly popular style Pope Benedict's thought. In a chapter on Scripture, Hemming declares that 'Benedict's underlying concern is for the ordinary believer to continue to have access to Scripture'. His worry is that interpretation of the Bible has been kidnapped by experts (whose language is scarcely comprehensible to ordinary mortals). By contrast, Ratzinger has written that the saints 'were often uneducated and, at any rate, knew nothing about exegetical contexts. Yet they were the ones who understood it best'. Hemming links this idea with an understanding of divine revelation that Joseph Ratzinger developed in his doctoral thesis, completed in 1957.

In ordinary talk, 'revelation' has been used as a synonym for Scripture, but Ratzinger, through working on the theology of St Bonaventure (1221–74), saw revelation as an act of God's self-communication to man. 'If Bonaventure is right,' he wrote, 'then revelation precedes Scripture and becomes deposited in Scripture, but is not simply identical with it. This in turn means that revelation is always something greater than what is merely written down.' That is not the language of a fundamentalist.

13 AUGUST 2005

Cicero's Eternal Law

Is the following statement about law reasonable, and what does it suggest about the person who wrote it? 'True law is reason, right and natural, commanding people to fulfil their obligations and prohibiting and deterring them from doing wrong. Its validity is universal; it is unchangeable and eternal. Its commands and prohibitions apply effectively to good men and have no effect on bad men. Any attempt to supersede this law, to repeal any part of it, is sinful; to cancel it entirely is impossible.' Perhaps it sounds as if it was written by some authoritarian Christian or moralistic Catholic. It tastes intolerant. But it was written by Cicero, who died 40 years before Christ was born. It comes in the *De Re Publica*.

A project to try to reach an agreed programme of what is right to do and what is wrong might be thought reasonable. Indeed, the human faculty traditionally called 'reason' has widely been thought capable of discerning a law applicable to all. That is exactly what, in the Christian tradition, has been known as natural law. To non-Christians, a rational approach should sound preferable to the dictates of divinely promulgated laws. The Ten Commandments seem uncontroversial – who would want to be a murderer, a thief or a liar? Yet religious rules on divorce, say, are not universally welcome. For all that, 'natural law' has somehow got a bad name. That beguiling philosopher John Haldane, in an essay in his new book *Faithful Reason* (Routledge), gives one explanation why. By some process of misunderstanding, people have attacked as 'absurd, cruel and superstitious' the principle of confining 'actions and policies to ones that do not interfere with natural processes'.

That is not what natural law means at all. Probably the confusion arose over 'artificial' as against 'natural' birth control. In 'natural law', though, the 'natural' refers to the natural light of human reason – as opposed to a supernatural lawgiver. Such is the incorrigibility of popular misapprehension, however, that the erroneous identification of natural law with 'natural processes' has more recently won support for natural law on the equally spurious grounds that it seeks 'natural' lifestyles rather than those spoiled by 'artifical' chemicals, pollutants and ecologically unfriendly practices.

This misunderstanding aside, problems remain in applying natural law. I notice among some believing Christians a fear of trusting the conclusions of reason, in the hope instead of relying directly on God's revelation. The trouble there is deciding what God's revelation means. If you do not use reason to decide its meaning, what authority do you choose instead? But another puzzle is: if law is discoverable by reason, how come people disagree about it so much? A corollary of that question is: how can toleration of pluralism be possible? Professor Haldane calls in aid (as a bookend to the nicely chosen quotation from Cicero) a concept explained by Thomas Aquinas, about the difference between 'speculative reason' (one might call it 'theoretical reason') and 'practical reason'. 'Since speculative reason is concerned chiefly with necessary things, which cannot be otherwise than they are, its proper conclusions, like universal principles, are invariably true. Practical reason, on the other hand, is concerned with contingent matters, about which human actions are concerned, and consequently, although there is necessity in general principles, the more we descend to matters of detail, the more frequently we encounter deviations.'

You can say that again. Thus different political parties try to attain the same ends by different means. Whether this distinction explains ethical pluralism I am not sure, but it is pleasant to have Cicero standing up for eternity and Aquinas for the mundane.

3 JULY 2004

Is Sex Love?

Is sexual love the same thing as the love of God, or are we just using the word 'love' to describe completely different things? That is the question the Pope addresses in his first encyclical, a letter addressed to the whole Church. It's an interesting question and quite a surprising one to attempt to answer as a priority. But Pope Benedict is perhaps an old man in a hurry. Just as the apostle John was said in his old age to have repeated 'God is love' as his sole message, so the Pope turns at once to the same question under the Latin title *Deus Caritas Est.* He doesn't duck the charge made against the Church of having spoilt sexual love for everyone: 'Doesn't the Church, with all her commandments and prohibitions, turn to bitterness the most precious thing in life?' he asks.

The Greeks, calling sexual love *eros*, saw it, the Pope notes, as a 'kind of intoxication' that overpowered reason with a 'divine madness' and sought to come near to divine power and supreme happiness. In several other religions, he writes, 'sacred' prostitution flourished in temples as an expression of fertility cults. But the temple prostitutes were not treated as human beings, or even as goddesses; they were exploited as a mere means of reaching this 'divine madness'. This dehumanizing use of *eros* was in reality not an 'ascent in "ecstasy"' towards the Divine' but 'a fall, a degradation'. In the modern world, he says, '*eros*, reduced to pure "sex", has become a commodity', and, with it, human beings have become commodified. By contrast, there is a kind of love called *agape* in Greek (*ahaba* in Hebrew), which 'involves a true discovery of the other'. As the people of Israel learnt: 'No longer is it a self-seeking, a sinking in the intoxication of happiness; instead it seeks the good of the beloved.' It is not so much an 'ecstasy' as an 'exodus', a 'journey out of the closed inward-looking self'.

But the Pope, who has never been married, is not tempted to say simply that *eros* is bad and *agape* good. He insists that they 'can never be completely separated'. Indeed, the Bible expresses God's love for his people in terms of married, sexual love. Even when his chosen people have committed 'adultery', God does not give them up: 'How can I give you up, O Ephraim? How can I hand you over, O Israel? . . . My heart recoils within me, my compassion grows warm and tender.'

One book in the Bible, the Song of Solomon, or the Song of Songs, is a poetic work about *eros*. Yet it was accepted by Jewish and Christian writers as also dealing with the relationship between God and human beings. Far from being comically unaware of the literal meaning of the book, spiritual writers realized that it was such a powerful way of describing relations with God precisely because the metaphor was based on sexual reality. There is no denying that the Bible, unlike the run of ancient religions, is fiercely in favour of marriage. It is more as if marriage is an image of God's real relationship with his people than the other way round.

Another prong of Pope Benedict's defence of the Christian approach to love is his reminder that when Christianity recognizes union with God as a high ideal, this union cannot be selfishly possessive. If Communion, the Eucharist, is *agape*, it leads to consequences for loving other people. 'Here the usual contraposition between worship and ethics simply falls apart,' the Pope writes. '"Worship" itself, Eucharistic Communion, includes the reality both of being loved and of loving others in turn.'

These others are our neighbours, and the second half of the encyclical discusses how they should be loved. It makes a useful stipulation about the duty of the state to establish a just order, without which rulers would be nothing but a *magna latrocinia* – a gang of thieves – as Augustine observed. That needs saying, but I was glad first to read Pope Benedict's idea that, fundamentally, 'love' is a single reality.

4 FEBRUARY 2006

11

Last Things

Return from the Grave

Tobit was exiled to Nineve, in what we now call northern Iraq. He was known for his almsgiving, and, as he related, 'If I saw any of my nation dead, or cast about the walls of Nineve, I buried him'. In doing this he risked death himself. Burying the dead is reckoned as one of the corporal works of mercy. It is a strange act to be called merciful, for burial is no help to the dead, who are already in a better (or worse) place. Yet the virtue of burying the dead, and the wickedness of treating them with contempt, is widely recognized in differing cultures. In Britain even those who admit to little religious belief retain a sensitivity about dead bodies. Unlike their counterparts in Continental Europe, British newspapers and television cannot show pictures of dead or mutilated bodies. In television footage of the charred bodies of the four American contractors killed in Fallujah, they were disguised with pixillations, as if they were obscene.

Some viewers have wondered if it was something to do with Muslim belief that the crowd hacked and displayed those unfortunate men's remains. Yet the contrary is true. They were maltreated after death out of hatred because such treatment ought not to be done. An obvious parallel was the dragging of two British soldiers from their car in Belfast in 1988 by a mob that beat them, shot them and left their bodies exposed on the road. Such behaviour is not sanctioned by Christian teaching. Burial is the practice of Christians, as Thomas Browne noted in his agreeable seventeenth-century prose, and 'though they stickt not to give their bodies to be burnt in their lives, detested that mode after death; affecting rather a depositure than absumption, and properly submitting unto the sentence of God, to return not unto ashes but unto dust againe'.

Browne knew enough of Muslim belief to explain that they too avoided cremation, expecting a 'trial from their black and white Angels in the grave'. This obscure reference is to the belief that the fearsome angels Munkar and Nakir will question the dead, and on those who answer unsatisfactorily the earth will lie heavy until the last judgement. The Koran leaves no more doubt about the resurrection of the dead and the last judgement than does Christian belief. '*Tuba mira spargens sonum per sepulchra regionum*', says the Christian devotional hymn *Dies Irae*; the loud trumpet will gather all before the throne of God. The day when they will hear a mighty blast, says the Koran, that will be the day of resurrection (Sura 50.37). Some faces that day will beam, looking towards their Lord; and some faces that day will be sad and dismal (Sura 75.22). The fate of the wicked is to be cast into hot blasts and boiling water in a darkness of pitchy smoke. Once upon a time, the wicked prospered, and they persisted in their crimes, saying: 'What, when we die, and have become dust and bones, shall we then indeed be raised?' (Sura 56.44).

Islam tends to frown on speculative theology, lest it become the work of the devil, distorting the revelation of God. But the religion is strong on law – the things to be done. And there is a clear connection between what is to be done with dead bodies and the expectation of the resurrection and last judgement. In Christianity there is a great deal of theologizing, and not much agreement. But the most obvious reasons for respecting the body, dead or alive, is first that it 'is the temple of the Holy Ghost' (1 Corinthians 6.19), and secondly that this body is the one that will rise again.

St Paul, later in the same letter to the Corinthians, uses a rhetorical figure that seems to argue backwards: 'If there is no resurrection of the dead, then Christ has not been raised; if Christ has not been raised, then our preaching is in vain and your faith is in vain.'

Christ's rising is what the Christian faith celebrates tomorrow in the greatest of its festivals, Easter.

10 APRIL 2004

Soul and Body

What do I think my soul is? A squidgy lump of ectoplasm somehow haunting my body? My deepest heart? The immortal lodger in a corporeal house of flesh? People still place tremendous importance on their notion of the soul. A symptom of this is an unresolved row about whether worshippers at church should answer the versicle 'The Lord be with you' with the response 'And also with you', or with 'And with your spirit'. The latter is a more literal translation, but modern liturgists tend uneasily to feel that spirits and souls belong to an obscurantist, dualistic past, and these days it is you or me that counts.

A very interesting historical survey of ideas of the soul has just been published by Rosalie Osmond, a writer and educationist. It is called *Imagining the Soul* (Sutton Publishing) and it takes as much note of the images of poets and painters as of the theories of philosophers.

Certainly, one may entertain several inconsistent ideas of the soul. This is nothing unique to the soul, for we talk of the sun rising, sinking and setting while simultaneously picturing earth turning and going round the sun. Rosalie Osmond makes the very good point that a concept of soul is a datum among different cultures; it hasn't required proving. The idea is 'deeply bound up with our very humanity. We are mortal, and we know we are mortal. It is a fact that we find profoundly disquieting. "*Timor mortis conturbat me.*" It is also what sets us apart from the rest of nature. Added to this, we have the ability to conceive, in some dim way at least, of eternity'. These two notions of mortality and eternity pull at our concept of the conscious self.

Their historical origins oblige Christians to be open to ideas of the soul held by the ancient Hebrews. When Israel was exhorted to 'love the Lord thy God with thy whole heart, and with thy whole soul', the Hebrew word *nephesh*, translated as 'soul', has the connotation of will; it also means 'life' (Lev. 17.11). In the Gospel, when Jesus says 'What shall it profit a man, if he shall gain the whole world and lose his soul?' the word used is *psyche*. That is Greek, since the Gospels were written in the lingua franca of the Middle East. The word was familiar to Homer. To him it meant both the life that was within a man and also the shade or phantom that survived in Hades. In a way the Homeric idea of *psyche* was not so different, as far as it went, from that of Jews in New Testament times, to whom the soul could be life or spirit or one's very being. But the philosophers ensured that the ambiguity natural in language became split into entrenched positions. Plato had pictured the soul as a prisoner of the body. If Aristotle regarded it as the informing principle of the living creature, what becomes of it when the organism dies?

Dante on his guided tour of Hell sees and speaks to men and women as they were in life. But Dante knew in theory that disembodied souls were invisible, and had no natural power to see or hear. He was writing in the *Divine Comedy* as a poet. Reason might conclude that a soul consisting of intellect and will – both capable of immaterial operations, of knowing intellectually and loving freely – is not susceptible to material decay. But after surviving the body it would have a pretty thin time of it. Once reliant on the senses to know what is going on and to communicate with others, it would, after the death of the body, neither see nor hear, nor be able to receive ideas from other persons. Only if, as Christian belief promises, it is made capable of seeing God is the soul saved from the shady half-life expected by Homer or Old Testament prophets. Even then, if the soul is the very principle and form of the body, it will not return to full working order until being reunited – according to that much neglected clause of the Creed 'the resurrection of the body' – with the corporeal reality for which it was first made.

31 JANUARY 2004

A Song to the End

Michael Mayne retired to Salisbury in 1996 after ten years as the Dean of Westminster. He thought he had written enough books, so set about putting together, without thought of publication, an account of his *cantus firmus*, a metaphor from music. The idea came from early church music, plainchant, which had a single line of melody. From the twelfth century onwards, harmonies began to be added to this *cantus firmus* 'fixed song', culminating in the glorious polyphony of Byrd in the sixteenth century. Higher and lower voices wrapped round the tenor that 'held' the *cantus firmus*. Michael Mayne quoted a comment on Bach, that in his music 'a theme can unfold inexorably through difference, while remaining continuous in each movement of repetition, upon an infinitely infinite surface of varied repetition'.

Using this metaphor, Mayne went on to assert his belief that 'the creation is an endless sequence of variations on the unchanging theme of God's creative love'. For him this meant 'not simply a vague concept of the transcendent, but that of the incarnate and affirming God: the Christlike God of the Word made flesh'. This *cantus firmus* metaphor of God's wholehearted love was one, Mayne noted, that Dietrich Bonhoeffer had written about while facing execution. 'Shortly after I had written all this in my confident retirement,' Mayne was to recall, 'the cancer struck.' It was cancer of the jaw. Mayne began to keep a diary as an honest account of the 'questioning country of cancer', and it is this, added to those personal introductory thoughts on the *cantus firmus*, that has now been published as *The Enduring Melody* (Darton, Longman and Todd).

On 4 July 2005 a biopsy confirmed the cancer, and details of a long, intricate operation were planned out. The next day he wrote: 'Morning Psalm, 56: "Whenever I am afraid, I will put my trust in you . . . for what can flesh do to me?" Try to relay it from head to heart.' Ten days later he wrote: 'Calmer now, but occasional moments of panic which, just by snapping its fingers, can at once obliterate the solid ground of trust and confidence I strive for.' Friends rang and wrote to him. 'The most succinct card, from a Roman Catholic friend, reads: "My God, what a bugger!" Spot on.'

There was an operation, pain, radiotherapy, the buying of a three-wheeled electric scooter, exhaustion. 13 November: '3am: "I can't go on." 8am: "I'll go on." Later I realise that these are the unconscious echo of the final words of Samuel Beckett's *The Unnameable* in the character's struggle between despair and hope. Epistle set for this Sunday, which I read from bed looking out at the distant spire of the cathedral where Alison [his wife] and so many friends are gathered for the Eucharist, is 1 Thessalonians 5.1–11. The last two verses read, Christ "died for us so that awake or asleep we might live in company with him. Therefore encourage one another, build one another up – as indeed you do."'

Around the feast of the Ascension this year, Mayne knew that further surgery was impossible, radiotherapy couldn't be repeated and that chemotherapy could buy only a few more months. He wrote: 'To die with gratitude for all that has been, without resentment for what you are going through, and with openness towards the future, is the greatest gift we can leave those who love us and who are left behind.' In conclusion he quoted his old friend John Austin Baker: 'He who holds me in existence now can and will hold me in it still, through and beyond the dissolution of my mortal frame. For this is the essence of love, to affirm the right of the beloved to exist. And what God affirms, nothing and no one can contradict.'

Michael Mayne died last Sunday.

28 OCTOBER 2006

The Victorian Way

Some readers have written in to *The Daily Telegraph* to say that they did not want to know so much about the Pope's sickness when he was dying or see so much of his dead body afterwards. Others wanted more. It is a matter of sensibility. In the past the British have been very eager to read every detail of the deaths of famous men. Albert's death commanded yards of print. I have in my bathroom a splendid photograph of Gladstone dead on his bed, dressed in an academic gown, with his hands carefully folded to conceal the finger he had many years earlier blown off by accident.

Nothing, perhaps, presents the flavour of Victorian death in London so well as a little book by Canon John Morris, of Westminster Cathedral, entitled *Cardinal Wiseman's Last Illness*. It must have sold, for my copy is the second edition of 1865, and Wiseman had only died in February of that year. Wiseman, Cardinal Archbishop of Westminster since 1850, had been more or less unwell from 1854 onwards. A man of natural energy, he had become corpulent and suffered from diabetes and heart failure. His legs began to be inflamed. Carbuncles appeared on his body. He was to die of erysipelas of the face – a streptococcal infection of the skin that would these days be cured with antibiotics, unless it was a resistant strain.

For Wiseman it meant prostration, painful operations without anaesthetic and the growing certainty of death. Throughout everything he remained cheerful, addicted to the ceremonial of the Church and eager to unite his sufferings with those of Jesus Christ his redeemer. It is an extraordinary narrative, and Canon Morris, who was in his room for days and nights, had no hesitation in setting down 'even those things that I heard from him in confidence'. 'I have always tried to fight against my cowardice,' Wiseman told Morris the night before another operation, in the last month of his life. 'Many years ago I determined never to call anything pain, or mention it until it was unendurable.' The author then gives Wiseman's account of being operated on for carbuncles on his back by Italian surgeons five years before, using scalpels and caustic. 'When I knew it was to be done, I sat on the chair, with my hands over the back, and laid my head on them. I couldn't help giving two great gasps; but Monsignor Manning, who was outside, never heard anything. You know they cut so deep. They thought that I was so quiet they could not have done enough and there must be more to cut. The dressings were worse than the operation – harder to bear. They burnt away, and thought there was mortification [necrotized flesh] because I kept quiet.'

Wiseman received the most up to date scientific medicine – which did nothing to cure him and only increased his pain. An unlooked-for attack came from nocturnal hallucinations, which Wiseman recognized for what they were. 'I had the strength to know that they were illusions,' he told his doctors the next morning. 'But I feel that the time might come when I should not have this strength. I therefore want you to tell me exactly how I am.' In one episode, when a nun was bathing his swollen carbuncular eye with ice water to soothe it, he had an experience common among those in pain of feeling dissociated from the experience. 'Reverend Mother,' he said. 'Please bathe my eye, or your eye, or somebody's eye, whose-ever it is, for I am sure it does not feel like mine.' One February morning, 'at a quarter past seven, he asked what o'clock it was. At half past seven I said to him, "I am going to say Mass for you – for a happy death. You can hear it from where you are." He answered: "Thank you. God bless you!" I do not know that he spoke again.'

9 APRIL 2005

The Death of the Pope

When the Pope was taken to hospital this week, television and newspapers, out of a vestigial sense of propriety, veered away from actually mentioning the risk of his dying that night. That would have been bad taste. The taboo of death takes the place of other absolute prohibitions in liberal western mores. Pope John Paul has no such inhibitions, and spoke about death in a recent audience. 'We often seek to ignore this reality in every possible way,' he said, 'distancing the very thought of it from our horizons. This effort, however, apart from being useless, is also inappropriate. Reflection on death is in fact beneficial because it relativizes all the secondary realities that we have unfortunately absolutized, namely, riches, success and power.'

Karol Wojtyla, as Pope John Paul was christened, was nine when his mother died. His only brother died when he was 12. His father died when he was 20. 'I never felt so alone,' he recalled. So the Pope had no unrealistic idealization of death. As a forced labourer in Nazi-occupied Poland he had seen too much of it. One of his first acts as Pope was to kneel and pray at Auschwitz.

It is clear that he has pondered the subject not only as a teacher of doctrine but also as a mortal man. 'On this reality the Word of God offers us, although gradually, a light to illumine and comfort us,' he said on the eve of the millennium, an anniversary that prompted him to think of the action of providence in the history of the world and in his own life history. He escaped death before he became a priest, let alone Pope. In 1944 he was knocked down in the dark by a German lorry and lay seriously ill for a fortnight. But of course the event that spectacularly almost ended his pontificate in its third year was the assassination attempt in St Peter's Square on 13 May 1981. It was very close. The bullet missed a major artery by a whisker. Two years later,

Pope John Paul visited his Turkish would-be assassin, Mehmet Ali Ağca, in prison. He calmed Ağca's fears that 'Our Lady of Fatima' (on whose feast day the murder attempt was made) would in vengeance pursue him to an early grave. The Pope explained that he should not be afraid of Mary, a figure after all venerated by Muslims, who loved all people.

Shortly afterwards, John Paul explored suffering and death in an encyclical letter, *Salvifici Doloris*. Death, he wrote, 'is often awaited even as a liberation from the suffering of this life'. But it is impossible, he said, 'to ignore the fact that it constitutes as it were a definitive summing-up of the destructive work both in the bodily organism and in the psyche'. In that sense it is bad. Yet if death was originally aligned with evil, it was transformed by the death and resurrection of Christ. As a consequence, St Paul could speak of 'various sufferings and, in particular, of those in which the first Christians became sharers "for the sake of Christ". These sufferings enable the recipients of that letter to share in the work of the Redemption, accomplished through the suffering and death of the Redeemer.'

It was that task of sharing in Christ's redemptive suffering that the Pope set himself, seeing his physical deterioration and sickness as part of his vocation. He accorded suffering and death a cosmic significance. 'In the terrible battle between the forces of good and evil, revealed to our eyes by our modern world,' he told the readers of his letter, 'may your suffering in union with the Cross of Christ be victorious.'

Salvifici Dolores was completed on the feast of Our Lady of Lourdes, and it was at Lourdes 20 years later, on 15 August 2004, that the Pope spoke with feeling of the fact that he would never return to the shrine. 'I feel with emotion,' he told the crowd, as tears wetted his cheek, 'that I have reached the end of my pilgrimage.'

5 FEBRUARY 2005

Getting Out of Hell

The Archbishop of Canterbury, speaking to a Christian festival
in the fields of Gloucestershire the other day, mentioned that
Muslims might go to heaven, even if 'no one comes to the Father
except by Jesus'. I suppose it would have caused more controversy if he had said they were all going to hell, the only alternative destination. It is funny how quite secular people, while placid
about the idea of heaven and not much feeling the need to do
what God asks, nevertheless become quite indignant at the idea
that they of all people should go to hell.

Someone who has been reconsidering the possibility of hell,
and of going there, is Eamon Duffy, an influential interpreter of
the late Middle Ages to our own. 'The thought of losing God
should make our flesh crawl, our souls turn sour,' he writes in his
new book *Faith of Our Fathers* (Continuum). 'It mostly doesn't,
however, and that is why the tradition has piled on the agony, why
the flames and flesh-hooks have been imagined, just to get across
to us how devastating, how agonising, such a loss would be.'

I used to assume, as perhaps most people do, that in the
Middle Ages everyone went in great fear of hell, painted as it was
on their church walls or by their parsons' sermons. Dr Duffy's
extraordinary book, *The Stripping of the Altars*, convinced me that
the ordinary Englishman of the fifteenth century lived in confident hope of heaven, as long as he pursued his religious duties
and avoided deadly sins. He remained anxious to avoid the pains
of purgatory through prayers and good works. For our own era,
'the century of Auschwitz and Belsen needs no picture language,
no painting on a wall, to convince it of the reality and horror of
evil'. Certainly, Dr Duffy allows that the concentration camp com-
mandant might be a twisted, hapless being who deserves our pity
more than our anger. But we can judge actions, he says, if not
people, and we need to be clear that the feeding of the gas
chambers is damnable 'if we are to fight it, or more, if we are not
to join in it ourselves'. For him, hell is believable 'because we can
imagine ourselves choosing it'. It is not a question 'about what
God is capable of, but what we human beings are capable of'.
And, as he observes, the recorded words of Jesus insist on 'the
possibility of absolute loss, of spiritual and moral disaster'. There

is no inevitability about our response to God or to other people. 'Hate and fear, as well as love and trust, are close to hand.'

In theory it is simple enough to see that if someone simply won't be saved, then he must go to hell. But it is not much consolation. In his book *Dare We Hope That All Men Be Saved?*, the theologian Hans Urs von Balthasar wrestled with both the possibility of hell and his great reluctance to see anyone consigned to it. He was infuriated by glibness in either dismissing hell or being happy at people going there. An interesting chapter in Balthasar's short book assembles some extracts from the diaries of Maurice Blondel (1861–1949) in which he considers Jesus Christ who 'made himself to be sin for us' in St Paul's words, suffering a hellish experience expressed in that cry 'My God, my God, why hast thou forsaken me?'. One has to be very careful here, for there are all sorts of mistakes to be made in considering Jesus's sufferings. He was not damned, he was not a sinner, and he was not separated from God. But 'he made himself to be sin, knew the ultimate forlornness, felt as if he were obliterated', Blondel wrote. 'He no more did away with hell than with sin and death.'

No, but when the sinless one takes the effects of sin upon himself, and the immortal one undergoes death, then the Psalm (22) that begins 'My God, my God, why hast thou forsaken me?' can reach its conclusion: 'All the ends of the world shall remember and turn unto the Lord.' The transition is not made easily or comfortably, nor merely by saying a word. If God does not let any particular person go to hell, it is not because he is too feeble to allow it, rather that he has gone to hell and back to prevent it.

11 SEPTEMBER 2004

Trees of Armageddon

In R. H. Benson's strange novel about Antichrist, there is a scene where the Pope, who has taken refuge in the Holy Land, asks a Syrian priest what they call the place they have reached among the palm trees. 'That is Megiddo,' he says. 'Some call it Armageddon.' Many have not needed the current crisis in the Middle East to suspect that the end of the world is upon us. Benson, who died as the First World War began, wrote *Lord of the World* in 1907, a decade after Wells' *The War of the Worlds*. It is a futuristic fantasy of quite a different flavour.

Benson got it wrong when he predicted a world of silence, muted by rubber and subterranean speedways. But he got some things frighteningly right, not just trivially, as with the 'volors', fast airships fulfilling the role of our helicopters. In an early scene in the novel, he shows how well he can depict new attitudes being taken for granted. A politician's wife witnesses a volor crash, and an injured man falls practically at her feet. She is upset to see a priest push through the crowd and say something over the man in a language she cannot understand. When the men from the euthanasia service arrive and put the wounded man out of his misery, she breathes a sigh of relief. Benson predicted a kind of disciplined ultramontane Catholic Church shrinking into a city of 'saints' in Rome, until Rome is destroyed by volor bombing and the death of 30,000 fleeing refugees. In Benson's imagination, details such as an ascetic breakfast of coffee remained, like the Latin language, almost a touchstone of the true Church.

In his end-time world, humanitarianism has become the dominant 'religion' of a Europe squeezed between the blocs of America and the Eastern Empire. Mabel, the anti-heroine who had witnessed the volor accident, later finds herself explaining to her dying mother how a new ideal has superseded her old superstitions. 'You said just now that you wanted forgiveness of sins', she tells the old lady. 'Well you have that; we all have it, because there is no such thing as sin. There is only crime. And then Communion. You used to believe that you were made a partaker of God; well, we are all partakers of God, because we are human beings. Don't you see that Christianity is only one way of saying all that?' But the old woman is deaf to reason and only cries out for a priest. Her last agony is cut short by euthanasia.

Into this world of humanist consensus enters a political leader of protean attractions. One day a new coin is minted. 'On one side was the familiar wreath, with the word "fivepence" in the midst.' On the other were the words in Esperanto, the common language of the modern world: 'Julian Felsenburgh, la Prezi-

dante de Uropo'. Benson, decades before the totalitarian cults of
Stalinism, Hitlerism or Maoism, depicts Felsenburgh as an
increasingly cultic figure. From his spellbinding oratory before
breathless crowds, profile-writers recollect his saying: 'A man who
believes in himself is almost capable of believing in his neighbour', and: 'No man forgives; he only understands', and: 'It
needs supreme faith to renounce a transcendent God'.

The humanism that Felsenburgh embraces begins to acquire
the trappings of a parody of religion. Benson imagines them as
something like the rites of the goddess Reason after the French
Revolution. Felsenburgh himself has a genocidal streak, for while
preaching peace and tolerance, he starts to explain the use of
'extermination as an instrument that might be judicially used in
the service of humanity'. To this leader, who unites the world's
warring blocs, are attributed 'all those titles hitherto lavished on
imagined Supreme Beings'. He is 'the Son of Man, for He alone
is perfectly human'. By now, the reader realizes, along with the
last Pope (whom Benson wisely make an Englishman, Percy
Franklin, taking the name Silvester III), that this leader is no
other than Antichrist.

It is easy to find flaws in R. H. Benson's novel, but it not only
appeals strongly to the imagination, it foretells attitudes to the
supernatural which, if not yet dominant, are accepted in whole
subcultures of Britain today.

22 JULY 2006

All About Rapture

So one day soon people are going to wake up and find that all the
Christians have been softly and silently taken away. It's called
'The Rapture'. There will follow seven years of tribulation – for
the ones left behind, that is. It sounds like science fiction, doesn't
it? Indeed, a bestselling series of ten novels by Tim LaHaye and
Jerry B. Jenkins, starting with *Left Behind: A Novel of the Earth's Last
Days* (1995), has sold in almost *Harry Potter*-ish millions.

Yet the *Left Behind* publishing phenomenon reflects the
remarkable fact that many – perhaps eight million – in the

United States really believe The Rapture is coming, probably soon. Makes sense, they say, what with this terrible world violence and Israel surrounded by hostile nations.

The Rapture is part of a package known as pre-millennial dispensationalism. The idea is apocalyptic – based carefully on the book of Revelation in the Bible – and declares that history is divided into epochs or dispensations, and we're running into the last times now. The 'pre-millennial' bit means that, before Christ reigns on earth for a thousand years, the faithful remnant of 'heavenly people' will be snatched up to heaven. The 'earthly people' will stay, and eventually 'Israel' will recognize Christ as the reigning Messiah. To many pious Protestants and Catholics, this sounds completely bananas. Where is any such thing hinted at in the Bible? Dispensationalists will point to 1 Thess. 4.16–17: 'The dead in Christ will rise first; then we who are alive, who are left, shall be caught up together with them in the clouds to meet the Lord in the air.' From the phrase 'shall be caught up' in Latin – '*rapiemur*' – comes their technical term Rapture. That is all very well, but most Christians happily leave unresolved the fine details of the Second Coming, in which they declare their belief in the words of the Nicene Creed: 'He will come again in glory to judge the living and the dead.'

Many dispensationalists have a habit of particularizing phrases in the book of Revelation, so that 'locusts' are interpreted as helicopters, or the 'bow' of Antichrist as intercontinental ballistic missiles. In mainline Christianity, eschatological beliefs about the end do exist, even if they are not highlighted. After all, the coming of the Kingdom of Christ is prayed for in the Lord's Prayer ('Thy kingdom come'). But it is generally seen as, in a way, already amongst us. The one act of Christ reconciling all men to God somehow telescopes time; the followers of Christ are already part of his Kingdom.

So where does this Rapture business comes from? If one man can be held responsible, it is John Nelson Darby (1800–88). He founded the separatist sect that became known as the Plymouth Brethren. He insisted on a division between the 'earthly' Israel and the 'children of God under grace'. From him can be traced the support for Zionism that perhaps surprisingly is championed by 'fundamentalist' Christians in America. Even the rebuilding of the Temple in Jerusalem and the resumption of animal sacrifices are expected there.

Since the 1830s there has been a sort of family tree in North America by which these ideas have been handed down through generations. Some were spread by Cyrus Ingersoll Scofield (1843–1921), whose *Scofield Reference Bible* sold more than five million copies. Later popularizers of The Rapture included Charles Ryrie, author of *Dispensationalism Today* (1965) and C. C. Carlson, in his *The Late Great Planet Earth* (1970), which has sold 35 million.

Belief in The Rapture in its dispensationalist sense might seem harmlessly eccentric. But it is notable that, from the Marcionists of the second century to the Fifth Monarchy Men of the 1660s, obsessive and individualistic interpretation of apocalyptic Scripture has led to the splitting of Christians into sects – and not seldom outbreaks of blinkered violence.

24 APRIL 2004

Index

Abrahamic religions xvi
abstinence from meat 2, 96
Adam
    children of 40
    depicted at Chartres 98
    Jesus as new Adam 57
    naming creatures 27, 59, 98
    raised from grave 57
Alcock, John 32
Alexander, Frances 111
Ambrose, St 67
Andrewes, Lancelot 53
angels
    at death 75
Anointing of Sick 74, 162
Anscombe, G. E. M.
    and Cambridge 28
    on Eucharist 72
Anson, Peter 90
Antichrist 87, 163
Aquinas, Thomas, *see* Thomas
Ark of Covenant 43
Ark of Noah 122, 123
Arnold, Matthew 49
Augustine, St, of Hippo
    on creation 27
    on just government 150
    on prayer 57
    against suicide 129
    on Trinity xvi, 143
Averroes (Ibn Rushd) 132

Bach, J. S. 110
Baker, Augustine 46
Baker, Henry 110
Balthasar, Hans Urs von 161
baptism
    and death of Jesus 67, 74
    infant 69
    Trinitarian 68

bats in church 99
Baxter, Richard 82
Beatitudes, Community of 1
Becket, *see* Thomas
Bede, St 43, 98
Beeson, Very Rev Trevor 37
beggars 13
bells 16
being, joy of 47, 50, 78
Benedict XVI, Pope 145, 148
Bennett, Frank 37
Benson, R. H. 161
Bernardine of Siena, St 33
Bethlehem
    and Eucharist 19
    and Incarnation 46
Bible
    in Anglo-Saxon world 43
    Authorized Version 43, 53, 64
    birds in 97
    Douai version 135
    and fundamentalism 145
    inclusive language 64
    interpretation in Antioch and
        Alexandria 79
    and revelation 146
    Septuagint version 136
    Vulgate version 43, 136
Bolton, William 32
Boniface, St 6
Book of Common Prayer, *see* Prayer
    Book
Booth, Cherie 49
Boyd, Ian 50
Bradley, Ian 110
Bridges, Robert 110
Brooks, James 22
Brown, George Mackay 70
Brown, Michelle P. 43
Browne, Thomas 151

Index

Bruno, St 32
Burrows, Ruth 55

Calabria, St Giovanni 81
Campion, St Edmund 93
Carlyle, Aelred 91
cat and fiddle 103
cathedrals
    Canterbury 80
    Chester 37
    Ely 32
    Exeter 103
    Girona 26
    Lincoln 35
    Norwich, St John's 28
    Santo Domingo de la Calzada 100
    St Alban's 104
    St Paul's, London 106
    Southwark 53
    Wells 103
    Westminster 36
Caxton, John 32
Charlton, William xi
Charterhouses
    Burgos 19
    Chartreuse 32
    London 30, 32
    Parkminster 30
Chesterton, G. K. 47, 48, 115
chickens
    in Chaucer 138
    in church 100
Christianity
    in Britain xv
    persecuted 128
Christmas see feasts
Church
    Body of Christ 20
    community 19
    unity of 81
churches
    furnishings: altar 20, 86; altar-rails
        106; brasses 101; dossals 115;
        lectern 86; misericords 103;
        reredos 21; windows xiv
    garnishing of 21
    God's houses 19
    locations: Antony, Cornwall 105;

Beverley, Yorks 103; Cambridge
    27; Clynnog Fawr, Gwynned 106;
    Clodock, Hereford 106; Eller-
    burn, Yorks 99; Fenny Stratford,
    Bucks 5; Gunby, Lincs 102;
    London: Bartholomew the Great
    32; Longstanton, Cambs 28;
    Northfleet, Kent 22; St Ives,
    Huntingdon 28; Oxford: St Mary
    54; Paray-le-Monial, Burgundy
    105; Paris: St Denis 35; Stoke
    D'Abernon, Surrey 101; Trump-
    ington, Cambs 102; Warbleton,
    Surrey 103; Yattendon, Berks
    110
    night opening of 25
Cicero 147
Cloud of Unknowing 46
Confession
    absolution 82
    at death 74
copes 33
coronation of James II 24
Corrigan, Dame Felicitas 77
cosmos
    biblical 26
    Ptolemaic 42
Coster, Will 105
Cottingham, John 141
Cox, Edward Young 21
Craig, John 105
creation 27
Cross
    Helena and 26
    Persian capture of 79
    sign of the Cross 70
    of St Andrew 23
    of St George 23
    in the world 49
Curtis, Geoffrey 31
Cuthbert, St
    and eagle 98
    Lindisfarne 43
    tomb of 24

Darby, John Nelson 164
deans 37
Dearmer, Percy 115

death
  in baptism 67, 74
  and burial 151
  and the Eucharist 73
  of Jesus 72
  of Pope John Paul II 73, 158
  Sister Death 75
  Stevenson and 49
  of Wiseman, Nicholas 156–8
Dickens, Charles
  and baptism 17
  and bells 17
dogs
  on brasses 102
  in church 105
dog-tongs 106
Douai 35
Douglas, Mary
  on abominations 3
  on abstinence 3
  on animals 108
  on ritual xi
  on sacrifice 122
dragons 102, 103, 104
Duffy, Eamon
  on fasting 3
  on hell 160
Duvernay, Pauline, later Mrs Lyne-
    Stephenson 28

Easter, *see* feasts
Edward the Confessor 24
Edward I meets Sauma 83
elephant 103
Eliot, T. S. 53
Elisabeth of the Trinity, St 55
Elizabeth I
  and bells 17
Ellsberg, Robert 59
embroidery 26, 34
Escrivà, St Josemaria 87
Eucharist
  presence of Jesus 72
  sacerdotal 106
  as Viaticum 73
Evans-Pritchard, E. E. 8
Extreme Unction, see: Anointing

fasting 2
feasts
  All Souls 6
  Annunciation 33
  Assumption 9
  Christmas 21
  Easter 67, 152
  Hallowe'en 6
  St Stephen 82
  Visitation 67
ferret 107
fish 2
flags 22
Forster, E. M. 27
Fox, George 20
Francis of Assisi 75
Frazer, James 141
Freud, Sigmund 141

Gardner, Gerald 7
Geldart, Ernest 22
George, St 23
Girona, embroidery 26
Gladstone, W. E. 156
Guadalupe (Mexico) 85
God
  Emmanuel, God with us 19, 43
  foreknowledge of 137
  goodness of 58–9, 139
  is xvii, 135
  love xvii, 149
  names of xvi, xvii, 33, 135
  Pantocrator 26
  providence of 57, 60, 97, 158
  Trinity xvi, 46, 140, 142
  unity of xvi, 133
  unknowable 46
  See also Holy Spirit; Jesus Christ
Godiva, Lady 62
Googe, Barnaby 9
Greene, Graham 92
Gregory, St 89

Haldane, John 147
Hallowe'en *see* feasts
happiness 59
hell 160
Hemming, Laurence Paul 146

Henley, W. E.   58
Henry III   25, 104
Henry VIII   30
Herbert, George   18
Heseltine, Peter   102
Hilary, St   113
holiness
   of God   xvi
   of places   20
   pursuit of   87, 88
Holy Spirit
   depicted as dove   26, 145
   dwelling in men   20, 152
   inspiration by   145
   praying in men   51
   and the sick   74
Homilies, Book of   111
Hooker, Richard   138
Houghton, John   30, 32
Howells, Herbert   110
Hubert, St   106
Hulagu   83
Huxley, T. H.   137

icons
   of Jesus in Gethsemane   56
   of the Trinity   46
Ignatius St, Loyola   62
Iraq
   Christians   15, 84
   Church of the East   82
   Karbala   119, 122, 124
   and Tobit   151
   Yazidis   28
Islam
   almsgiving   118
   Ashura   122
   in Britain   xv
   dhikr   125
   God in   118
   jahiliyah   134
   judgement of the dead   152
   Koran   118, 130
   Mohammed   119
   persecution of   127
   pilgrimage   118
   prayer   62, 117, 118, 127
   Ramadan   117, 118

sacrifice   121
saints   124
sharia   119, 134

James I
   and baptism   70
James II   24
Jerome, St   43
Jerusalem
   Holy Sepulchre   46
   New   75
Jesus Christ
   and altar   20
   death of   72, 74, 161
   in Eucharist   73
   in human heart   44
   human will of   79
   IHS   32
   Kingdom of   164
   prayer to   52
   as priest   71
   in the womb   xv, 113
   union with sufferings of   157, 159
   Word   43, 144
John the Baptist   95
John of the Cross, St   55
John Paul II, Pope
   death of   73, 158
   in Mexico   85
Johnson, Samuel   73
Jones, Peter   95
Josquin Desprez   116
Juan Diego, St   84
Judaism
   in Cordoba   131
   and idea of God   135
   in London, 1663   4; 2003   10;
      2005   133
   Passover   12
   Sabbath   10
   in Yemen   96
Julian of Norwich   45
Jung, Carl   140

Kempis, Thomas à *see* Thomas
Kenny, Anthony   137, 143
Kenny, Michael   14
Kirchmeyer, Thomas   9

laity 88
Lancaster, William 40
Lapidge, Michael 80
Laud, William 53, 106
Lee, Laurie 20
Lewis, C. S.
   on David Lindsay 41
   and Giovanni Calabria 81
liberation theology 85
Lindisfarne Gospels 42
Lindsay, David 41
lion 102
liturgy
   of Addai and Mari 71
   for animals 107
   choral 87
   and furnishings 92
   inexplicable xiii
   Syro-Malabarese 115
locusts 95
Luff, Alan 115

MacDonald, George, 42
Magnus, St 70
Maimonides, Moses 131
Manichaeanism 41, 113
Mary, Virgin
   Assumption of 9
   distrust of 87
   of Guadalupe 85
   invocation of 116
   of Lourdes 159
   and Pope John Paul II 159
   pregnancy 113–14
Manning, Henry Herbert 89
Martin, St 5
Marvell, Andrew 67
Matarasso, Pauline 46
materialism 47
Matthew Paris 104
Maximus, St 79
Mayne, Michael 154
Melchizedek 70
Meri, Josef 124
Methodism 44
   and holiness 87
Mexico 1, 84, 92
Milbank, John 143

monks, eastern, in Rome 79
morality
   consequentialism 72
   inherited 39
   natural law 147
   Stevenson's 47
   theft 77–8
   Utilitarianism 72
Morris, John 156

Naogeorgus 9
Nestorianism 84
Newman, John Henry
   on animals 107
   and baptism 70
   on beggars 14
   and Thomas Aquinas 142
   translator of Andrewes 54
Nichols, Aidan 143
nihilism 50

Opus Dei 88
Orosius 81
Osama bin Laden 83

Pancras, St 80
panther 102
Paradise
   entry to 75
   rivers of 26
Parry, Hubert 110
pelican 102, 103
Pepys, Samuel 4
Philo 136
Pickstock, Catherine 143
Polycarp, St 128
prayer
   Christ-centred 56, 62
   during the day 52
   God's action 55, 57
   and Gospels 56, 61–2
   imaginative 52
   Lord's Prayer 51
   mental 51–2
   openness to God 56
   petition 58, 60
   presence of God 61
   Teresa of Avila on 55

thanksgiving 54, 58, 156
time for 56
verbal 51–2
Wesley on 44
Prayer Book
of Edward VI 34
of 1559 70
of 1662 69, 70, 112
Pro, Miguel 92
Psalms 63
Pym, Barbara 111

Rapture 163
Rassam, Suha
rebuses 32
redemption 57, 114, 159
relics 16
in Constantinople 79
of St Pancras 80
reparation 40
resurrection of the body 67–8, 152, 154
Riley, Athelstan 116
Rogers, Nicholas 28
rosary 62
Roud, Steve 6

sacrifice
of Eucharist 71, 133
human 7
in Islam 121
of Melchizedek 71
to pagan deities 96
redemptive 41
Temple 71, 133, 165
white bulls, by Yazidis 29
Sauma 82
Saward, John 113
Schillebeeckx, Edward 72
Schools, 'faith' 129
Sharp, Cecil 115
Sibthorp, Richard 86
Smith, Alexander McCall 39
Smith, John, sebaptist 69
Solidarity 85
soma 109
soul 153–4

Southworth, St John 35
Stevenson, Robert Louis 47
superstition 123

Taylor, Richard 4
Teresa, St, of Avila
on prayer 55
Tertullian 70
Theodore, St, of Tarsus 79
Thérèse, St, of Lisieux 15
Thomas Aquinas
Chesterton on 49
on Eucharist 144
on practical reason 148
on Trinity 142
Thomas Becket
hair shirt 35
tomb 24
Thomas à Kempis 44
Thomas, George 77
Trollope, Anthony 112
Trott, Michael 86

unicorn 102
Utley, Tom 113

vegetarianism 96
Victoria, Queen
sketches ballerina 28

Wade, John 113
Ward, Keith 58
water 68
Waugh, Evelyn 92, 137
Wesley, John
Westminster Abbey
tombs 24
waxworks 37
White, Victor 140
Whittier, John Greenleaf 109
Wicca 7
Williams, Ralph Vaughan 115
Williams, Rowan, Archbishop of
Canterbury
on Carthusians 31
in Hooker, Richard 139
and hymns 114, 115

poetry of 45
  on salvation by Jesus 160
Willis, Browne 5
Wiseman, Nicholas 86, 156–7
witchcraft 8

Yazidis 28
Yelton, Michael 90

Zoroastrianism 29